THE PHOENIX PATH

THE PHOENIX PATH

RISING FROM THE ASHES OF NARCISSISTIC ABUSE

EMILY CLARK

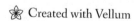

CONTENTS

Free Gift   6

1. Introduction   9
2. The Flames of Narcissism   21
3. The Smoldering Coals   34
4. Caught in the Inferno   48
5. The Ashes   63
6. Sparks of Change   77
7. Rising from the Ashes   92
8. The Flight   106
9. The Phoenix's Plumage   116
10. Soaring High   135
11. The New Horizon   146
12. The Phoenix's Flight   155

A Personal Request from the Author   165
About the Author   167
Unlock Your Full Healing Potential   169

FREE GIFT

To assist you on your healing journey, I've crafted this FREE companion resource to the book.

You can get instant access to **The Phoenix's Toolkit** by either clicking the link or scanning the QR code below.

This bonus is 100% free with no strings attached. You don't need to provide any personal information except your email address (so that I can send it to you).

This interactive workbook allows you to put the theory into practice and tailor your recovery strategies to your specific experiences and situations.

To get your bonus, go to:
subscribe.reprynted.com/phoenix-path-bonus

Or scan the QR code below

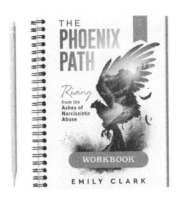

This **workbook** and **journal** is designed as a companion to the main book. It provides you with practical exercises, reflective prompts, and guided journaling sections tailored to each chapter of the book. This **interactive resource** aims to further facilitate the healing process by allowing you to actively engage with the material, reflect on your personal experiences, and track your progress over time.

Personalized Journey: The toolkit allows you to customize your healing journey, ensuring that your unique experiences and feelings are addressed.

Practical Application: It translates the theoretical and informational content of the book into actionable steps, ensuring that you can apply what you learn.

Progress Tracking: By regularly journaling and completing exercises, you can visibly see your progress, reinforcing motivation and commitment to recovery.

1

INTRODUCTION
THE PHOENIX PATH

In the heart of ancient lore, the Phoenix, a magnificent bird of flaming splendor, captures our imagination. This mythical creature, cloaked in radiant plumage of gold, crimson, and royal purple, is renowned for its singular life cycle. Unlike other birds, the Phoenix does not merely live and die. Instead, when its long life nears its end, it ignites into a brilliant spectacle of fire and heat, reducing itself to a humble mound of ashes. But this is not the end. From those ashes, a new Phoenix, more vibrant and resilient than before, emerges, reborn and ready to start its life anew. This cycle, a ceaseless pattern of death and rebirth, encapsulates an enduring testament to resilience and transformation.

This book is called "The Phoenix Path" because, like this mythical bird, we can rise from the ashes of our past experiences. Even when we are ground down to our most basic elements by the fire of narcissistic abuse, we hold within us the capacity to regenerate, to come back stronger and more resilient than we ever imagined.

When we find ourselves lost in the destructive cycle of narcissistic abuse, we might feel that our lives have been reduced to ashes, our spirits dampened, and our hopes smothered. But let's remember the Phoenix, who teaches us that even from the darkest ashes, we can rise. We can reclaim our life, regain our strength, and rekindle the flame of our spirit.

This is not a promise that the journey will be without trials and tribulations, but it is a promise that the journey is possible. The path of the Phoenix is not merely one of survival, but one of transformation and rebirth. I invite you to join me on this journey, to understand, heal, and ultimately rise above the ashes of narcissistic abuse, embodying the spirit of the Phoenix.

Narcissistic abuse, a term you might have encountered before, could sound both vague and intensely personal. If you're reading this book, chances are you've already been touched by this destructive pattern of behavior. You may have been left questioning your own reality, your worth, or even your sanity. I want you to know that what you've experienced is real, and your emotions, no matter how complex, are valid and important.

Narcissists, at their core, are individuals characterized by an inflated sense of self-importance, a deep need for excessive attention and admiration, and a lack of empathy for others. But behind this mask of extreme confidence lies a fragile self-esteem that's vulnerable to even the slightest criticism. These individuals can be charming, charismatic, and magnetic, making it easy to be drawn into their orbit.

In relationships, narcissists typically employ a love-bombing phase at the outset, in which they make you feel like the center of their world, giving you intense attention and admiration. However, this initial phase of idealization is often followed by a period of devalua-tion, where they start to criticize, belittle, and gaslight you, causing you to doubt your perceptions and value. This damaging cycle can make leaving the relationship and recovering from it quite challenging.

Narcissistic abuse can take many forms, including emotional, psychological, financial, and sometimes physical abuse. It's not limited to romantic relation-ships; it can happen between family members, friends, or coworkers. The abuse often manifests as coercive control, manipulation, blatant disregard for your feel-ings, constant criticism, and gaslighting - a tactic used to make you question your own sanity. The narcissist uses these methods to gain and maintain power over you, making you feel dependent, worthless, and alone.

If these descriptions resonate with you, know this: You are not alone, and what you are experiencing or have experienced is not your fault. Acknowledging that you're in an abusive relationship is the first step towards healing. Just like the Phoenix, you too can rise from these ashes, stronger and more resilient. This is your path, and it begins with understanding the nature of the beast you're dealing with - narcissistic abuse.

The fallout from narcissistic abuse is multifaceted and far-reaching, touching every aspect of a victim's life. From your mental well-being to your physical health, your relationships, and your very understanding of who you are, nothing escapes unscathed.

On a psychological level, narcissistic abuse can lead to a range of mental health problems. A study published in the Journal of Psychiatric Research reports that individuals exposed to narcissistic abuse are more likely to experience depression, anxiety, and post-traumatic stress disorder (PTSD). This abuse can also instigate a deep-seated self-doubt, often manifested as the victim questioning their worth, abilities, and even their sanity.

One of my clients, Sarah, spent years in a relationship with a narcissistic partner. She entered my office, a shadow of her former self, consumed with anxiety and depression. Sarah expressed feelings of being lost and disconnected from her own life, as if she were watching herself from a distance. She described a once vibrant world that had become bleak and desolate, where she felt invisible and insignificant.

Physically, the stress caused by such an abusive relationship can have significant health repercussions. Chronic stress can result in a weakened immune system, sleep disorders, and even cardiovascular issues. The constant state of hyper-vigilance, waiting for the next emotional assault, takes a toll on the body.

Emotionally, victims often find themselves on a rollercoaster, vacillating between love and fear, hope and despair. They may feel addicted to their abuser, caught in a vicious cycle of abuse and reconciliation. This intense emotional turmoil can leave the victim feeling empty, numb, and detached from their own feelings.

The social impact is equally destructive. Narcissists are masters of isolation tactics, often steering their victims away from family and friends to heighten their control. Victims may also withdraw socially out of shame or fear of judgment, creating a sense of isolation and loneliness.

These effects, as harrowing as they are, should be recognized not to instill fear but to validate your experiences. It's important to understand that you are not 'overreacting' or 'imagining things'. The pain you feel is real, and it's a direct result of the abuse. But remember, like the Phoenix, you hold within you the ability to rise above this, to heal, grow, and reclaim your life.

The road to recovery after surviving narcissistic abuse can be compared to a long, winding path. It's rarely straight, often bumpy, and occasionally shrouded in fog. But just as with any journey, each step you take, no matter how small, brings you closer to your destination. In this case, the destination is a life free from the grips of narcissistic abuse, a life where you are the author of your own narrative.

Recovering from narcissistic abuse involves several key stages. First, you must recognize and acknowledge the abuse. This step may seem simple, but it often involves unlearning the manipulations and distortions you've been subjected to. You must then fully understand and accept the impact the abuse has had on your life, your health, your relationships, and your self-esteem.

Once you have done that, you can start working on healing from the trauma. This usually involves therapeutic interventions like counseling or psychotherapy, as well as self-care routines, setting boundaries, and gradually rebuilding your self-esteem.

The journey also includes breaking free from the narcissist. This can be an emotionally challenging step as it may involve cutting ties with someone you have deeply cared for. But it's an essential step in regaining control of your life and wellbeing.

Finally, there is the process of rebuilding your life, rediscovering who you are outside of the abuse, and learning to foster healthier relationships.

Each of these stages is a crucial step on your path to recovery. Each one comes with its challenges, its setbacks, but also its victories. This journey, while difficult, is indeed possible, and it's one of the most rewarding endeavors you can undertake. Imagine the joy of rediscovering your worth, the freedom of living without walking on eggshells, the empowerment of setting boundaries and expecting respect.

This journey is about more than just survival; it's about transforming your life. It's about rising from the ashes, stronger, braver, and more resilient than before. The path may be steep, but the view from the top, the view of a life reclaimed, is worth every challenging step. Remember, as your guide on this journey, I'll be here with you every step of the way, helping you navigate through the fog, over the bumps, and around the bends. Like the Phoenix, you too can soar high above the flames of your past.

This book is your comprehensive guide, a roadmap if you will, designed to help you navigate the journey of recovery from narcissistic abuse. It is created to serve three primary purposes. Firstly, to help you understand the intricacies of narcissistic abuse, who narcissists are, and how they operate. Secondly, to assist you in breaking free from the abusive relationship, equipping you with the necessary tools and strategies to safely and effectively disengage. And lastly, to guide you as you rebuild your life post-abuse, fostering resilience, self-love, and healthy relationships.

The book is organized into twelve chapters, each addressing a crucial aspect of understanding, surviving, and overcoming narcissistic abuse.

Chapter 1, "Introduction to the Phoenix Path", is the one you are reading now. We've just explained why the book is called The Phoenix Path, what narcissistic abuse is and its impact on our daily lives.

Chapter 2, "The Flames of Narcissism: Identifying the Narcissist," delves into defining narcissism, understanding narcissistic behaviors, and uncovering the motives behind the abuse.

Chapter 3, "The Smoldering Coals: The Role of Empathy in Narcissistic Abuse" delves into the interplay between narcissists and empaths, detailing why empathic individuals are often targeted and offering strategies for their protection.

Chapter 4, "Caught in the Inferno: Understanding Narcissistic Abuse," explains how narcissistic abuse operates, detailing the cycle and exploring its psychological and emotional impacts.

Chapter 5, "The Ashes: Acknowledging and Accepting the Impact," underscores the importance of acknowledging the abuse, exploring the depths of the damage it has caused.

Chapter 6, "Sparks of Change: Preparing for the Journey Ahead," emphasizes the significant decisions necessary for initiating change, mental preparation for healing, self-care, and setting boundaries.

Chapter 7, "Rising from the Ashes: Breaking Free from Narcissistic Abuse," provides guidance on how to disengage from a narcissist, with advice on developing an escape plan and discussing legal and social considerations.

Chapter 8, "The Phoenix's Plumage: Rediscovering and Nurturing Your Personal Interests Post Abuse" emphasizes the rejuvenation of personal interests and hobbies after escaping a narcissistic relationship, guiding readers towards self-discovery and healing through individual passions.

Chapter 9, "The Flight: Rebuilding Life Post Abuse," offers tips on rebuilding your life, rediscovering personal identity, maintaining No Contact or Low Contact, and the importance of a support system.

Chapter 10, "Soaring High: Healing and Moving Forward," explores holistic healing approaches, the importance of self-love, and how to navigate new relationships after narcissistic abuse.

Chapter 11, "The New Horizon: Avoiding Narcissists and Fostering Healthy Relationships," helps you identify red flags in new relationships, build and maintain healthy relationships, and ensure personal growth and continued self-care.

Finally, Chapter 12, "The Phoenix's Flight: A Conclusion and A New Beginning," recaps the journey through the Phoenix Path, encourages continued growth and resilience, and provides final reflections and next steps.

Remember, every step on this path is a significant move towards reclaiming your life. You are not alone in this journey. Together, we will rise from the ashes.

I still remember the day Laura walked into my office. Petite and pale, she had a haunted look in her eyes that I had seen far too often. As she began sharing her story, a tale of endless manipulation, of mental and emotional torment by someone who had claimed to love her, my heart ached. Laura's story was not new to me. As a psychologist, I've counseled many victims of narcissistic abuse, helping them navigate their pain, confusion, and fear. But Laura's resilience, her determination to break free, was what really struck me. It reminded me of why I chose this path.

You see, my interest in narcissistic abuse is not only professional but also personal. I have had my own experiences with narcissism and its devastating effects. Growing up, I lived under the shadow of a narcissistic parent. I've felt the guilt, the confusion, and the despair that comes with living in an environment where your self-worth is constantly undermined. This experience, as painful as it was, led me to my calling - to help others on their path to recovery.

Laura's journey, like so many others I have been privileged to witness, wasn't easy, but it was inspiring. Through our sessions, I watched her rediscover her strength, reclaim her identity, and redefine her boundaries. Witnessing her transformation reminded me of the legend of the Phoenix, that mythical bird that rises from its own ashes, stronger, brighter, and more powerful than before. It was Laura's journey, along with many others, that inspired the concept of the Phoenix Path - the journey of healing and rebirth that each survivor of narcissistic abuse embarks on. And it's that very journey that this book, and our collective stories, are all about.

As we come to the close of this introductory chapter, I want to remind you, dear reader, that just as the mythical Phoenix rises from the ashes, so can you. The journey may seem daunting, the path full of uncertainties, but know this—you are not alone. I've walked this path, as have countless others before us, and while each journey is unique, the destination remains the same: a life rebuilt on the foundations of self-love, self-respect, and empowerment.

This book is more than just a guide—it is a torchlight in the darkness, illuminating the way forward. It's okay to feel overwhelmed, to be afraid, and even to stumble. It's okay to ask for help. And it's perfectly okay to take time to heal. What matters most is that you take that first step on this path, however small it might seem.

Narcissistic abuse leaves scars, but remember, a scar is not just a mark of pain—it's also a symbol of survival. It's a testament to your strength, to your resilience. And though it might not feel like it now, you possess an incredible ability to rise, to heal, to rebuild, and to thrive. Just like the Phoenix, you too can transform your deepest pain into your greatest power.

As you turn the page, remember this is not just a book —it's your companion on the journey ahead. A journey that might be challenging but is undoubtedly rewarding. I invite you to embark on this transformative journey, the Phoenix Path, with me. Together, we will rise. Together, we will soar.

Here's to your journey, dear reader. Let the flight of the Phoenix begin.

2

THE FLAMES OF NARCISSISM
IDENTIFYING THE NARCISSIST

Every one of us, at some point, has looked in the mirror and admired what we saw. Maybe it was after an especially good hair day or when we managed to perfectly wing our eyeliner on the first try. In moderation, this self-appreciation is not just healthy, it's necessary. It speaks of self-esteem and confidence—two traits that help us navigate the world around us.

However, when self-admiration crosses certain boundaries, when it becomes the driving force behind one's actions and behaviors, and when it blinds an individual to the needs and feelings of others, we move from the realm of healthy self-esteem to the land of narcissism.

Now, when I say narcissism, I'm not talking about the occasional self-centered moment or a healthy dose of self-confidence. I'm referring to pathological narcissism —an inflated sense of self-importance and a deep-seated need for admiration that's paired with a distinct lack of empathy for others.

Psychology and psychiatry recognize this as Narcissistic Personality Disorder (NPD). According to the Diagnostic and Statistical Manual of Mental Disorders (DSM-5), NPD is characterized by a pattern of grandiosity, constant need for admiration, and a lack of empathy, often accompanied by a sense of entitlement, frequent envy of others, and arrogant behaviors or attitudes.

It's important to remember that NPD is a diagnosed disorder, not a label for anyone exhibiting selfish behavior. NPD is far more severe, pervasive, and damaging, both to the individual living with it and to those in their sphere of influence.

The world of a pathological narcissist is like a fortress where they are the king or queen, and everyone else is either a loyal subject or a threatening usurper. But beneath this grand exterior often lies a fragile self-esteem, vulnerable to the slightest criticism.

Understanding this is key to understanding the narcissist in your life. It's the first step on your Phoenix Path —your journey from the ashes of narcissistic abuse to a renewed, resilient self. With this knowledge, we can begin to understand the 'why' behind their behavior, which in turn equips us to deal with it more effectively.

Just as there are many breeds of dogs, each with its unique characteristics, there are different types of narcissism, each with its own distinct behaviors and impact on relationships. In the animal kingdom, understanding a creature's traits can mean the difference between cohabitation and conflict. The same holds true when dealing with narcissists. Knowing the 'breed' you're dealing with can greatly affect how you navigate your interactions with them.

Overt Narcissism: This is the type most people think of when they hear the word "narcissist." Overt narcissists are hard to miss. They're the life of the party, the center of attention, the one everyone looks at when they enter a room. They have an inflated sense of self-importance and often brag about their accomplishments, real or imagined. They are dominating, often belittling others to keep themselves elevated. In relationships, they can be excessively demanding and uncaring of their partner's needs.

Covert Narcissism: The covert narcissist, also known as the vulnerable narcissist, is the wolf in sheep's clothing. Unlike their overt counterparts, covert narcissists often appear shy, self-effacing, and sensitive to criticism. However, they harbor grandiose fantasies and feel entitled to special treatment. They may play the victim and use passive-aggressive tactics to manipulate others. In relationships, they may drain their partners emotionally with their constant need for reassurance and validation.

Malignant Narcissism: This is narcissism at its most dangerous. Malignant narcissists combine the worst aspects of narcissistic and antisocial personality disorders. They are grandiose, lacking in empathy, often sadistic, and have a paranoid streak. They manipulate and exploit others without remorse. In relationships, they can be abusive, both emotionally and sometimes physically.

Communal Narcissism: This type of narcissist builds their grandiose image by associating themselves with communal goals or groups. They like to see themselves as generous, nurturing, and altruistic. However, their seemingly good deeds are primarily a means to gain admiration and praise. In relationships, they may demand appreciation and often use guilt as a manipulation tool.

Vulnerable Narcissism: Vulnerable narcissists are hypersensitive to criticism and often lash out or withdraw at the slightest hint of it. They alternate between feelings of grandiosity and unworthiness. In relationships, they can be highly controlling to protect themselves from perceived threats.

Recognizing these types is crucial in understanding the dynamics at play in your relationship with a narcissist. Keep in mind that narcissists may not fit neatly into

THE FLAMES OF NARCISSISM

these categories; they can exhibit behaviors from more than one type. However, having this framework can provide valuable insights into their behaviors and motivations, helping you navigate your Phoenix Path journey more effectively.

It's been said that knowledge is power, and when it comes to recognizing narcissistic behaviors, this couldn't be more accurate. Being able to identify these behaviors not only validates your experiences but also equips you with the understanding you need to navigate through or even away from a toxic relationship.

Here are some common behaviors and manipulation tactics of narcissists:

Gaslighting: This is a psychological tactic used to make you question your reality. Narcissists might deny things happened, contradict your memories, or accuse you of misunderstanding. For example, after a heated argument, they might completely deny any wrongdoing or even the argument itself. This can make you question your memory, perception, and even sanity.

Stonewalling: This tactic involves the narcissist refusing to communicate or cooperate. They might ignore you, give you the silent treatment, or dismiss your concerns. For instance, when you attempt to discuss their hurtful behavior, they might simply walk away or stare at their phone, refusing to engage.

Idealize-Devalue-Discard Cycle: Narcissists often engage in a three-stage relationship cycle. First, they put you on a pedestal, showering you with compliments (idealize). Then, they belittle you, criticize you, and make you feel worthless (devalue). Finally, they discard you, either physically by leaving or emotionally by withdrawing their affection.

Lack of Empathy: Narcissists are notoriously lacking in empathy. They struggle to understand or share the feelings of others, making their relationships one-sided and emotionally draining.

Sense of Entitlement: Narcissists believe they are inherently deserving of privileges or special treatment. They expect others to go out of their way to fulfill their needs without reciprocating.

Constant Need for Admiration: Narcissists thrive on the admiration of others. They may seek compliments and react negatively to criticism or perceived slights.

Manipulative Behavior: Narcissists are masters of manipulation. They can twist situations, play the victim, or use guilt to influence others' actions and feelings.

Blame Shifting: When something goes wrong, a narcissist will always find someone else to blame. They struggle to accept responsibility for their actions, often pinning their mistakes on those around them.

Spotting these behaviors can be the first step in acknowledging that you're dealing with a narcissist. Remember, these behaviors are not reflections of your worth or character. They're manipulative tactics used by the narcissist to maintain control and avoid accountability. As we move forward on our Phoenix Path journey, we'll explore ways to respond and cope with these behaviors.

Understanding the motivations behind narcissistic abuse can provide a sense of clarity and context. But remember, comprehension doesn't equate to condonation; the aim is not to excuse or justify the narcissist's behavior but to equip you with knowledge and insight.

Fear of Abandonment: Beneath the bravado and grandiosity, many narcissists harbor a deep-seated fear of abandonment or rejection. This fear often stems from early childhood experiences and can trigger a desperate need to control their relationships. They may resort to manipulative tactics, such as gaslighting or guilt-tripping, to keep their partners feeling confused and off-balance, less likely to leave.

Need for Control and Admiration: Narcissists have a profound need for control and admiration from others. They crave the spotlight and want to be seen as superior. To maintain this facade, they may manipulate those around them into providing constant praise, even at the expense of the latter's self-esteem and wellbeing.

Lack of Empathy: Empathy—the ability to understand and share the feelings of others—is a key characteristic that narcissists lack. This lack of empathy allows them to treat others poorly without feeling remorse or guilt. It also makes it easier for them to exploit others to meet their own needs.

Insecurity and Fragile Self-Esteem: Despite their outward projection of confidence, narcissists often have fragile self-esteem and are highly sensitive to criticism. This insecurity can lead them to belittle or devalue others as a way of boosting their own sense of worth.

Sense of Entitlement: Narcissists often believe that they're special or superior, leading to a sense of entitlement. They believe they deserve more than others and should be treated preferentially, and they'll manipulate others to cater to their desires.

It's important to note that these motives—rooted in fear, a need for control and admiration, a lack of empathy, and a sense of entitlement—don't excuse or justify narcissistic abuse. Everyone has fears and insecurities, but it's how we choose to manage these feelings that define us. Understanding these motives isn't about fostering sympathy for the narcissist; it's about empowering you with knowledge. The Phoenix Path isn't about the narcissist—it's about you, your resilience, and your journey towards healing and rebirth.

As a psychologist, I've worked with countless individuals who've been ensnared in the toxic web of a narcissist. Time and again, I've been asked: "Why me? What made me a target?" I want to stress first and foremost, that anyone—irrespective of their personality, strengths, or weaknesses—can fall victim to a narcissist's allure. Their charm can be intoxicating, their manipulation, subtle and insidious. So if you've found yourself in this situation, please don't shoulder the blame.

However, over the years, my experience and research have led me to identify a few common threads. It's these threads—codependency, lack of boundaries, and low self-esteem—that can, at times, make some individuals more susceptible to narcissistic entanglement.

Codependency: Codependent individuals often prioritize the needs and feelings of others above their own, to the point of self-sacrifice. This characteristic is unfortunately appealing to narcissists, who are always looking for someone to feed their insatiable need for attention and validation.

Lack of Boundaries: Boundaries are the invisible lines we draw around ourselves to protect our physical, emotional, and mental wellbeing. Individuals who struggle to set and enforce boundaries often end up tolerating disrespectful or abusive behavior. Narcissists tend to push and cross these lines, gradually dismantling a person's sense of self.

Low Self-esteem: Individuals with low self-esteem often find it hard to believe that they deserve to be treated with kindness and respect. Narcissists prey on this vulnerability, using criticism and rejection to further undermine their victim's self-worth.

If you recognize any of these traits within yourself, know that it's not a mark of weakness, but an opportunity for growth. Identifying these factors is the first step toward change. Remember, the Phoenix Path is a journey of rebirth, a journey of turning these vulnerabilities into strengths. Throughout this book, I'll be right there with you, guiding you towards healthier relationships with others and, most importantly, with yourself.

Before we close this chapter, I'd like you to take a moment of reflection. Think about the people in your life and the relationships you have with them. Consider their behaviors, the dynamics of your interactions, and the feelings these relationships elicit within you.

Below, you'll find a brief self-assessment questionnaire. This isn't a diagnostic tool, but rather a guide to help you gain personal insight into your relationships. It might help you identify patterns that echo the narcissistic behaviors we've discussed in this chapter.

1. Does the person often dominate conversations, turning the focus on themselves?
2. Do they lack empathy and seem disinterested in your feelings or experiences?
3. Do they react intensely or defensively to criticism or perceived slights?
4. Do you often feel used or manipulated by this person?
5. Do they frequently belittle or devalue your accomplishments or aspirations?
6. Are they excessively concerned with their image and how others perceive them?
7. Do they use guilt, blame, or victimhood to manipulate situations to their advantage?
8. Have you noticed a cycle of idealization, devaluation, and discard in your relationship with them?
9. Do they make grandiose claims about their achievements or abilities, often without concrete evidence to back them up?
10. Do you feel emotionally drained or anxious after spending time with them?

If you've answered 'yes' to several of these questions, it's possible you may be dealing with a narcissistic individual. Remember, this questionnaire is not definitive but meant to help you reflect on your experiences and relationships.

Your feelings and experiences are valid. Your well-being matters. And if you've recognized the flames of narcissism in your life, know that you're already on the path to rising above them, just like the Phoenix.

As we wrap up this chapter, let's revisit what we've uncovered in the ashes of our journey. We started by understanding what narcissism is, separating it from the realm of healthy self-esteem and identifying it as a pathological condition. We learned about Narcissistic Personality Disorder (NPD) and discovered its presence may not always be overt, but can manifest in covert and less obvious ways.

We ventured deeper into the different types of narcissism – overt, covert, malignant, communal, and vulnerable. Each type, while distinct, shares a common thread: the capacity to disrupt and damage relationships. We explored specific behaviors, manipulative tactics, and psychological cycles characteristic of narcissistic abuse, such as gaslighting, stonewalling, and the relentless loop of idealization, devaluation, and discarding.

We sought to understand the why behind the narcissist's actions, delving into their fear of abandonment, their insatiable need for control and admiration, and their glaring lack of empathy. However, we reminded ourselves that understanding their motives does not excuse their behavior or diminish the pain it causes.

Then, we turned the spotlight on ourselves, discussing why some people become targets of narcissists. Factors like codependency, boundaries, and self-esteem can play a significant role, but remember, anyone can fall prey to a narcissist.

Finally, we turned introspective, with a self-assessment exercise to help you identify if there might be a narcissist in your life. Remember, this is not for diagnosis but for insight.

And now, we find ourselves at the end of this chapter, but on the brink of a new beginning. Identifying the narcissist in your life is the first and one of the most crucial steps towards healing. You are embarking on a transformative journey, the Phoenix Path. It's a path of understanding, resilience, and ultimately, rebirth. It's not an easy path, but remember, the Phoenix does not shy away from the flames; it rises from them.

So, keep going. Keep rising. Each page you turn, each chapter you begin, is a step forward in your journey. Understanding is the first key to transformation, and you've already unlocked the door. As we continue on this path, know that I am here with you, every step of the way.

Until the next chapter, my fellow Phoenix. Remember, the flames don't define us; it's how we rise that truly matters.

3

THE SMOLDERING COALS

THE ROLE OF EMPATHY IN NARCISSISTIC ABUSE

Empathy, in its simplest form, is the ability to step into someone else's shoes, to momentarily live their feelings and understand their perspective. It is a bridge of connection, a force that binds us together and makes us profoundly human. Empathy isn't just about feeling for someone—it's feeling *with* someone. This act of resonance, of truly being with another in their emotional space, sets the stage for deep interpersonal connections and mutual understanding.

Broadly, psychologists have identified two main forms of empathy: cognitive and emotional. Both play unique roles in our interactions, and understanding their nuances can deepen our appreciation for the complexity of human connection.

Cognitive Empathy: This refers to our ability to comprehend what another person might be feeling or thinking. In essence, it's like "mind-reading" but not in

34

the mystical sense. It's about perspective-taking, where we mentally put ourselves in another's situation and gauge their probable thoughts or feelings. Cognitive empathy doesn't necessarily involve any shared emotion; instead, it's an intellectual understanding. Research, such as that published in the journal "Neuropsychologia," has shown that specific brain regions like the medial prefrontal cortex are activated during cognitive empathic processes.

Emotional Empathy: Unlike its cognitive counterpart, emotional empathy is all about *feeling*. It's the visceral, emotional response we have to someone else's feelings, where we quite literally feel their pain or joy. When a friend shares heartbreaking news and you find tears streaming down your face—that's emotional empathy in action. It's this deep, shared emotional experience that often binds people together, creating a bond that transcends words. Studies, such as those appearing in the "Journal of Neuroscience," have linked areas like the anterior insula and anterior cingulate cortex to emotional empathy, highlighting the neural basis of our shared emotions.

Empathy plays a pivotal role in human relationships. It's the glue that holds friendships together, makes romantic relationships flourish, and even aids professionals in fields like therapy, healthcare, and customer service. It allows us to support, validate, and uplift each other. It's a foundation for trust, as when someone feels truly understood, they're more likely to open up, trust, and collaborate.

The inherent value of empathy in interpersonal relationships cannot be overstated. Research, including studies in the "Journal of Personality and Social Psychology," has consistently shown that empathy promotes pro-social behaviors, fosters trust, and can even play a role in conflict resolution.

In a world teeming with diverse experiences, cultures, and feelings, empathy is the universal language. It's the undercurrent of our shared humanity, bridging gaps and binding hearts.

At first glance, empaths and narcissists may seem like polar opposites. Empaths, with their deep well of compassion and innate desire to understand others, appear worlds apart from narcissists, who often exhibit a self-centered worldview. However, it's precisely this stark contrast in their emotional makeup that often draws the two together, creating a powerful, albeit frequently unbalanced, dynamic.

To better comprehend this magnetic pull, envision a dance. One partner—the empath—leads with open arms, eager to understand, heal, and connect. The other—the narcissist—steps forward with a longing to be seen, acknowledged, and, most importantly, admired.

Here's a closer look at this intricate interplay:

1. **Filling the Void:** Narcissists, despite their outward bravado, often harbor deep-seated insecurities and a hunger for validation. The empath, with their natural inclination to listen, understand, and validate, seems like the perfect match for a narcissist's needs. They provide the adoration and attention that narcissists crave.

2. **Healing Instinct:** Empaths have an inherent desire to heal and fix. They can sense the vulnerabilities lurking beneath a narcissist's confident exterior. Misinterpreting this vulnerability for genuine emotion, empaths might believe they can 'save' or 'heal' the narcissist, drawing them into the relationship even deeper.

3. **Chameleon-Like Adaptation:** Empaths, in their quest to harmonize and avoid conflict, may often adapt or downplay their needs. This pliability can be particularly appealing to narcissists, who prefer relationships where they can take center stage.

4. **The Validation Loop:** As empaths strive to please and comfort, narcissists receive the validation they seek. This forms a loop where the more an empath gives, the more the narcissist takes, perpetuating the cycle.

It's crucial to understand that this dynamic isn't about assigning blame or implying that empaths "ask" for such interactions. Empaths possess beautiful, rare qualities that can bring light and healing to countless lives. However, these very qualities, when not safeguarded, can also make them susceptible to those who might exploit their generosity and understanding.

The aim of delving into this dynamic isn't to criticize but to illuminate. Awareness is the first step to empowerment. Recognizing patterns allows for change, adjustment, and the cultivation of relationships that respect and honor the empath's profound gift.

Empathy is undeniably a gift, allowing individuals to forge deep connections, bring solace to the hurting, and inspire trust in others. Yet, like any gift, it comes with its set of challenges. When unchecked or misunderstood, this very ability can become an avenue for manipulation and exploitation.

Let's explore the nuances of this double-edged sword:

Emotional Overload: Empaths, in their quest to understand and resonate with others, often absorb the emotions around them. While this can lead to profound connections, it can also result in an overwhelming influx of emotions, causing emotional fatigue.

Example: Consider Sarah, a therapist. Her days are filled with listening to clients share their deepest traumas. While her empathic nature makes her an excellent counselor, she often finds herself carrying the weight of her clients' emotions long after her sessions end. Over time, this takes a toll, leading to burnout and emotional exhaustion.

The Rescuer Trap: The inherent desire to heal can sometimes push empaths into situations where they overextend themselves, trying to 'fix' or 'save' individuals, often at their own expense.

Example: Jake, with his kind-hearted nature, always finds himself attracted to people with problems. His most recent relationship was with a partner who struggled with addiction. Believing he could support and 'rescue' her, Jake ignored red flags, often finding himself in emotionally draining situations, which left him feeling used.

Vulnerability to Manipulation: Empath's genuine wish to understand and help can make them prime targets for manipulative individuals. Narcissists, in particular, can recognize and exploit this trait, using guilt, pity, or flattery as tools.

Example: Nina, a team leader, is known for her understanding nature. When a colleague repeatedly missed deadlines, he would confide in Nina about his personal problems as the reason for his delays. Wanting to help, Nina would often cover for him, not realizing she was being manipulated.

Neglecting Personal Needs: In their pursuit to assist others, empaths might sideline their needs, desires, or aspirations. Over time, this neglect can lead to feelings of resentment or a sense of lost identity.

Example: Ananya always put her family first. When her brother faced financial troubles, she offered her savings without hesitation. Years later, she realized she'd deferred many of her dreams, like traveling or buying a house, to cater to others.

Empathy's beauty lies in its authenticity, its raw and genuine ability to resonate with another's experience. However, it's essential to recognize the potential pitfalls that come with such an open heart. Awareness and understanding allow empaths to navigate the world with their gift, ensuring they enrich their lives and the lives of others without self-compromise.

Empathy, in all its beauty, is a precious resource. However, just as we wouldn't leave a treasured possession unprotected, we must also defend our empathic abilities against potential misuse. Below are some actionable strategies to help empaths shield their compassionate hearts from manipulation:

1. Set Clear Boundaries:

- **Definition:** Boundaries are like invisible lines that define what you find acceptable and unacceptable in your interactions with others.

- **Action Step:** Begin by recognizing your limits. What can you emotionally handle? How much time can you dedicate? Once acknowledged, communicate these boundaries to others and stick to them, even if met with resistance or guilt tactics.
- *Example:* If a friend consistently calls late at night, affecting your sleep, you might say, "I value our conversations, but I can't talk past 10 PM. Let's catch up at a time that works for both of us."

2. Practice Self-Awareness:

- **Definition:** This involves understanding your emotions, triggers, and reactions.
- **Action Step:** Regular self-reflection, journaling, or meditation can heighten awareness, helping you identify when you're being unduly influenced or manipulated.
- *Example:* If you always feel drained or anxious after interacting with a particular person, it might be a sign to reevaluate that relationship.

3. Educate Yourself on Narcissistic Behaviors:

- **Definition:** Recognizing the early signs of narcissistic tendencies can act as a first line of defense.
- **Action Step:** Read up on typical narcissistic behaviors, or consider counseling to better understand patterns of narcissistic abuse.
- *Example:* Beware of excessive flattery or love-bombing in the initial stages of a relationship. These could be tactics to win you over rapidly.

4. Prioritize Self-Care:

- **Definition:** This involves activities that rejuvenate your mind, body, and soul.
- **Action Step:** Dedicate regular time for activities you love, be it reading, nature walks, hobbies, or simply relaxing. Ensuring you're mentally and emotionally charged will reduce your vulnerability to manipulation.
- *Example:* If you're a nature lover, weekly hikes could be a way to recharge.

5. Seek Support:

- **Definition:** A trusted circle of friends, family, or professionals who can offer perspective and validation.

- **Action Step:** Build and maintain relationships with individuals who understand and value your empathic nature. They can provide insights when you're too emotionally involved to see clearly.
- *Example:* Joining a support group for empaths can be a source of shared experiences and coping techniques.

6. Trust Your Gut:

- **Definition:** Your intuition is a powerful tool in discerning genuine interactions from manipulative ones.
- **Action Step:** If something feels off or too good to be true, pause and evaluate. It's okay to step back or seek more information before proceeding.
- *Example:* If a new acquaintance is rushing intimacy, pushing for quick commitments, or dismissing your reservations, it might be time to slow down and reassess.

Being empathic in a world filled with varied intentions isn't always easy, but it's undoubtedly worthwhile. By implementing these protective measures, empaths can ensure they continue to spread their unique light without dimming their own.

After emerging from the shadows of narcissistic abuse, empaths might, for a fleeting moment, consider their deep sense of empathy as a liability. However, in the grand tapestry of human existence, it's this very empathy that threads beauty, connection, and understanding. Let's reclaim this magnificent gift and turn those scars into badges of resilience.

Empathy is not a weakness, but a superpower.

In the words of Dr. Brené Brown:

> Empathy fuels connection. Sympathy drives disconnection.

Empathy is a bridge that connects souls, a healing touch that mends wounds, and a mirror reflecting raw human emotions. While narcissists might exploit this quality, the fault lies not in empathy but in their misuse of it. Always remember, your empathy is a testament to your vast emotional landscape, not a sign of fragility.

Maya, an empath, had once been ensnared by Tom, a charismatic individual who later unveiled his narcissistic tendencies. Post the harrowing experience, Maya initially viewed her compassionate nature with skepticism. Over time, however, with introspection and support, she transformed her trauma into a mission. Maya now conducts workshops, guiding others like her, emphasizing the strength in vulnerability and the power of empathy.

Here are some practical steps to healing and reclaiming empathy:

1. Therapy and Counseling: A trained professional can offer coping mechanisms, validation, and healing strategies tailored to your experiences.

2. Empathic Communities: Engaging with fellow empaths can provide comfort in shared experiences and insights into handling overwhelming emotions.

3. Journaling: Documenting your journey can be therapeutic. It offers clarity, records progress, and acts as a testament to your resilience.

4. Mindfulness and Meditation: Grounding exercises can help empaths center themselves, especially when overwhelmed by external emotions.

5. Reaffirmation: Daily affirmations can reinforce self-worth. A simple mantra like "My empathy is my strength, and I wield it with wisdom" can be empowering.

> Our wounds are often the openings into the best and most beautiful part of us – David Richo

The journey might have its share of thorns, but it leads to a garden blossoming with wisdom, strength, and an even deeper appreciation for the beauty of empathy. The key is to remember that while narcissistic encounters may be a chapter in the book of an empath's life, they're not the entire story. There are countless chapters yet to be written, filled with growth, understanding, and love.

Empathy, the innate ability to step into another's shoes and feel their emotions as if they were one's own, is a rare and precious gift. Throughout this chapter, we've delved into the rich tapestry of empathy, from its inherent value to its potential vulnerabilities when confronted by the calculating dynamics of a narcissist.

Key Takeaways:

1. Empathy's Dual Nature: We've explored empathy in its cognitive and emotional dimensions, highlighting that it goes beyond mere understanding to deeply feeling and connecting with another's emotional state.

2. The Empath-Narcissist Dynamic: This magnetic attraction, a dance of opposites, arises from the deep-seated needs of both parties: one seeking validation and connection, the other, control and affirmation.

3. The Potential Pitfalls: While empathy is undeniably beautiful, it also has its challenges. Left unchecked, an empath's desire to help and heal can lead to emotional exhaustion, burnout, and susceptibility to manipulation.

4. Guarding the Empathic Heart: Setting boundaries, recognizing early signs of manipulation, and prioritizing self-care are essential for empaths to shield themselves from exploitation.

5. From Scars to Strength: Post-narcissistic abuse, the journey of healing is centered on recognizing empathy as a strength, a testament to one's vast emotional depth, and not a sign of fragility.

As we close this chapter, let us acknowledge and celebrate the profound depth and strength that lies in being empathic. Your empathic abilities are not only invaluable but are also much-needed in a world thirsting for genuine connection, understanding, and compassion.

Armed with knowledge, introspection, and the strategies discussed, you are now better equipped to navigate the world, cherishing your gift of empathy while also ensuring you remain protected from potential harm. Let every interaction, every experience, be a testament to the Phoenix's resilience and growth. Your empathic journey is one of strength, love, and unwavering spirit. Celebrate it, cherish it, and continue soaring high.

4

CAUGHT IN THE INFERNO
UNDERSTANDING NARCISSISTIC ABUSE

In the shadowed corners of intimate relationships, there exists a form of abuse that's as insidious as it is profound: narcissistic abuse. Often, it moves subtly, like smoke, leaving its victims in a state of confusion, doubt, and emotional turmoil. As we embark on this journey to understand its depths, remember that you are not alone, and there is hope in knowledge.

Narcissistic abuse is primarily emotional and psychological. Unlike physical abuse, where the signs might be visible, this form of abuse leaves scars on the psyche, invisible to the naked eye but palpable to the one enduring it. These internal scars can manifest in myriad ways: diminished self-worth, constant self-doubt, anxiety, and a persistent feeling of walking on eggshells.

It's essential to distinguish narcissistic abuse from other types of maltreatment. While all forms of abuse are unequivocally damaging, narcissistic abuse is characterized by a continuous assault on the victim's identity and self-worth. The abuser, driven by their deep-seated insecurities and need for control, systematically chips away at the victim's reality, a phenomenon commonly referred to as "gaslighting". This process can be so pervasive that the victim may begin to question their own perceptions, memories, and even sanity.

The covert nature of this abuse makes it particularly challenging to recognize, even for the victims themselves. Often, it's interwoven with moments of affection, kindness, and intimacy — a confounding blend of love and loathing. This interplay is purposeful, designed to keep the victim off balance and perpetually seeking the narcissist's validation.

One of the most heart-wrenching aspects of narcissistic abuse is the isolation it fosters. Victims may feel that they can't speak about their experiences because they seem so "ordinary" or "trivial" compared to overt forms of abuse. But the pain, the erosion of self, and the constant feeling of being "less than" are anything but trivial.

If you find yourself nodding along or feeling a resonance with what's described here, know that your feelings are valid, and your experiences are real. The journey of the Phoenix is one of rising from the ashes of adversity, and understanding is the first spark that ignites that transformative ascent.

The trajectory of a relationship with a narcissist often follows a predictable yet heartbreaking cycle. This cycle, although nuanced in its manifestations, generally encompasses three primary phases: idealization, devaluation, and discard. Each phase serves a specific purpose in the eyes of the narcissist and leaves a distinct mark on the victim.

Idealization Phase

Hypothetical Situation: Consider Sarah, a young woman who meets David at a mutual friend's gathering. David is charismatic, attentive, and seems genuinely interested in getting to know Sarah. He showers her with compliments, sends her thoughtful messages, and plans elaborate dates. To Sarah, it feels as though she's met her soulmate.

Real-Life Story: Jane, an actual patient from my practice, once shared, "When I first met Michael, it was like a fairy tale. He made me feel like I was the center of his universe. He'd often say we were 'meant to be,' and I genuinely believed it."

In the idealization phase, the narcissist creates a mirage of the "perfect" relationship. The victim is placed on a pedestal, made to feel special, unique, and loved like never before. This "love-bombing" is both intoxicating and disarming, making it hard for the victim to see any red flags.

Devaluation Phase

Hypothetical Situation: As weeks turn into months, Sarah starts to notice a shift in David's behavior. The same qualities he once adored in her are now sources of criticism. He becomes moody, unpredictable, and often lashes out over trivial matters. Sarah feels like she's perpetually walking on eggshells, trying to avoid David's next bout of rage or disdain.

Real-Life Story: Jane reflected, "A few months in, Michael's demeanor changed. I went from being his 'everything' to never doing anything right. He'd belittle me in front of friends, then apologize profusely later, leaving me constantly confused."

In the devaluation phase, the narcissist's true colors begin to show. The same person who once idealized the victim now sees them as deeply flawed. This phase is characterized by constant criticism, passive-aggressive behavior, gaslighting, and emotional manipulation.

Discard Phase

Hypothetical Situation: Sarah feels increasingly isolated, both emotionally and sometimes even physically, as David starts to distance himself. He becomes indifferent, often ignoring her or prioritizing other aspects of his life, making her feel disposable.

Real-Life Story: "Eventually, Michael lost interest," Jane recounted. "He'd often disappear for days, offering flimsy excuses. One day, he just said he didn't feel 'the spark' anymore and left."

In the discard phase, the narcissist often abandons the relationship, either physically or emotionally. They might start new relationships, further adding to the victim's pain. For the narcissist, the victim has served their purpose and is no longer of use.

This cycle is a harrowing experience, one that leaves deep emotional scars. But understanding it is the first step toward breaking free and beginning the healing journey, just as the Phoenix rises, renewed and resilient, from the ashes.

The art of narcissistic manipulation is anchored in a toolkit of specific tactics that disorient, disempower, and emotionally enslave the victim. These tactics are often subtle, making them particularly insidious. Let's delve into some of the most common ones:

1. Gaslighting

- **Definition:** A psychological manipulation tactic where the abuser makes the victim doubt their own reality, memory, or perceptions.
- **Example:** If Linda confronts her partner, Mark, about a lie she caught him in, he might respond, "That never happened. You're imagining things," or "You're always so paranoid and dramatic."
- **Impact:** Over time, repeated gaslighting erodes the victim's trust in their own memory

and judgment. This fosters dependency on the narcissist as the "reliable" source of truth, leading to feelings of confusion and self-doubt.

2. Triangulation

- **Definition:** This involves using a third person to validate the narcissist's viewpoint or to undermine the victim's self-worth.
- **Example:** John might tell his wife, Claire, "Even Mary agrees with me that you're too sensitive." Or he might flirt openly with Mary in front of Claire, instilling jealousy and insecurity.
- **Impact:** Triangulation creates divisions between the victim and others, further isolating them. It also serves to validate the narcissist's claims or behaviors, making the victim feel alone in their grievances.

3. Love-Bombing

- **Definition:** An overwhelming display of attention and affection towards the victim, especially during the early stages of a relationship or after a conflict.
- **Example:** After a disagreement, Alex might inundate Rachel with gifts, romantic gestures,

and promises of undying love, only to revert to his abusive ways once he feels she's securely back under his influence.

- **Impact:** Love-bombing creates an emotional roller coaster for the victim. The intense highs of affection make the subsequent lows and abusive behaviors even more confusing and painful, trapping the victim in a cycle of hope and despair.

4. Projection

- **Definition:** A defense mechanism where the narcissist attributes their own negative traits or behaviors onto the victim.
- **Example:** Emma, who is constantly unfaithful, might accuse her partner, Liam, of being the one who's cheating, even if he's shown no signs of infidelity.
- **Impact:** Projection shifts the blame from the narcissist to the victim, who may end up constantly on the defensive. Over time, the victim might internalize these accusations, leading to diminished self-esteem and a distorted self-image.

Understanding these tactics is akin to shining a light in the darkness of narcissistic abuse. With awareness, one can start to see the patterns, reclaim their reality, and protect their self-worth. The journey may resemble the path of the Phoenix, challenging yet transformative, leading to a renewed sense of self.

Narcissistic abuse is not merely a sequence of unsettling events; it's an insidious, soul-wrenching storm that can dismantle a person's psyche and emotional equilibrium. Like a forest fire that chars everything in its path, this form of abuse leaves scars that may not always be visible but are deeply felt.

1. Complex Post-Traumatic Stress Disorder (C-PTSD)

Unlike PTSD, which usually arises from a singular traumatic event, C-PTSD develops due to prolonged exposure to trauma, such as long-term narcissistic abuse. Victims might relive the emotional torment through flashbacks or nightmares, causing them to be in a state of perpetual alertness, awaiting the next round of emotional assault.

Symptoms: Emotional numbness, jumpiness, intrusive thoughts about the abuse, feelings of worthlessness, and difficulty in forming close personal connections.

2. Anxiety

Given the unpredictable nature of narcissists and their often volatile mood swings, victims live in a state of constant hyper-vigilance, always anticipating the next emotional ambush. Over time, this state of high alert can evolve into chronic anxiety.

Symptoms: Constant worry, rapid heartbeat, trembling, nausea, and obsessive thinking.

3. Depression

The repetitive devaluation by the narcissist can lead victims to internalize the negativity, making them feel trapped and helpless. The bleakness of the situation and a degraded sense of self-worth can culminate in depression.

Symptoms: Persistent sadness, fatigue, changes in appetite, feelings of hopelessness, and even suicidal thoughts.

4. Other Mental Health Implications

It's not uncommon for victims of narcissistic abuse to develop other psychological challenges, including:

- Dissociation: Feeling disconnected from oneself or the environment, as if watching life from the outside.
- Substance Abuse: Turning to drugs or alcohol as a way to cope with or numb the pain.
- Self-Harm: Engaging in self-destructive behaviors as a cry for help or a way to externalize internal pain.

CAUGHT IN THE INFERNO

It's crucial to understand that these reactions are not signs of weakness or an inherent flaw in the victim. Like the Phoenix, scarred by flames but destined to rise, every individual has an inherent resilience. Experiencing these feelings and symptoms is a testament to the profound impact of the trauma, not a character deficiency.

To anyone recognizing these symptoms within themselves, remember: you are not alone in this. Thousands have walked this path, bearing similar burdens. With understanding, support, and professional guidance, the journey towards healing and reclaiming oneself is not only possible but promised. Your ashes, though remnants of a painful past, contain the essence of your rebirth.

Over the years, countless individuals have walked into my therapy practice, each bearing the weight of their experiences. Though every story is unique, the threads of narcissistic abuse often weave a pattern that's tragically familiar. I'd like to share a couple of these stories, altered to preserve confidentiality, but powerful in their message of pain, resilience, and hope.

Laura's Story

Laura was a vibrant, young professional when she first met Mark at a community event. Mark was charismatic, attentive, and seemed genuinely interested in everything Laura had to say. He would surprise her with thoughtful gifts and leave notes in her lunchbox every day. However, as time passed, the notes that once spoke of love began pointing out what he perceived as her flaws.

Laura came to me, feeling like a hollow shell of her former self. Mark's criticisms and ridicule had infiltrated her self-worth. He isolated her from her friends, making her believe they were jealous of their "special bond." Every time she mustered the courage to leave, Mark would swing back to the sweet, doting partner she first met, promising change. But the cycle only continued.

It was in our sessions that Laura began to understand the nature of Mark's behavior. As she learned more about narcissistic abuse, she drew strength from her newfound knowledge. With support from therapy and reconnecting with loved ones, Laura finally broke free. Today, she is an advocate for mental health and uses her experience to help others recognize and escape toxic relationships. Her journey, though marked by pain, has transformed her into a beacon of hope for many.

Ethan's Story

Ethan was a retired military officer and the embodiment of strength. When he shared his story of being ensnared in a web of deceit and manipulation by his narcissistic partner, Jane, it was a stark reminder that narcissistic abuse knows no boundaries. Jane would oscillate between being affectionate and cold, using

Ethan's vulnerability against him. She often belittled his military service, labeling him as "damaged."

It was a surprise to many when Ethan started attending support groups for victims of narcissistic abuse. But he often said, "It was in the midst of understanding my wounds that I found my strength." With time, therapy, and the camaraderie of his support group, Ethan rediscovered his sense of self. He began volunteering at veterans' centers, combining his personal experience and military background to provide unique support.

Both Laura and Ethan's stories are testament to the Phoenix's journey. The flames of narcissistic abuse tried to consume them, but with understanding, support, and an indomitable spirit, they rose, more formidable and radiant than before. Their stories are not just tales of survival but of profound transformation.

In our journey of understanding narcissistic abuse, it's often helpful to pause and reflect on our own experiences. This self-assessment is a tool to help you identify patterns that may resonate with your relationships. Remember, this is a tool for reflection and not a formal psychological assessment.

Self-Assessment Exercise: Recognizing Narcissistic Abuse Patterns

1. Emotional Roller Coaster: Do you often feel like your relationship is an emotional roller coaster, with extreme highs and lows?

2. Walking on Eggshells: Do you frequently feel anxious about your partner's reactions, feeling like you're "walking on eggshells" to avoid conflict?

3. Constant Criticism: Does your partner often belittle or criticize you, sometimes under the guise of "joking"?

4. Isolation from Loved Ones: Has your partner tried to distance you from friends or family, or criticized those close to you?

5. Memory Doubts: Have you ever been made to doubt your memory or reality, being told events didn't happen the way you remember them?

6. Overwhelming Adoration: Did the relationship start with intense adoration, with your partner placing you on a pedestal?

7. Shift in Behavior: Have you noticed a stark contrast in your partner's behavior, from being extremely affectionate to cold and distant?

8. Control Over Decisions: Does your partner seek to control aspects of your life, such as how you dress, who you see, or financial decisions?

9. Feeling Drained: Do you often feel emotionally or mentally exhausted after interactions with your partner?

10. Fear of Abandonment: Does your partner use threats, directly or indirectly, about leaving you or harming themselves if you were to leave?

If you find yourself answering 'yes' to several of these questions, it might indicate patterns that are common in relationships characterized by narcissistic abuse.

Recognizing these patterns is an important first step. The path of the Phoenix begins with understanding. Remember, just as the Phoenix needs the flames to rise anew, our experiences, no matter how painful, can be the catalyst for profound transformation and growth.

If you resonate with many of the patterns described above, consider seeking professional support. A therapist or counselor can provide guidance tailored to your unique situation, helping you navigate the complexities of your experiences.

The journey through this chapter has been a deep dive into the labyrinth of narcissistic abuse. It's a realm often shrouded in confusion, pain, and self-doubt. Yet, with understanding comes empowerment. Just as the Phoenix rises from the ashes, transformed and radiant, you too possess the strength to rise above and heal from your experiences.

Narcissistic abuse may have darkened chapters of your life story, but it doesn't define you. The path forward is one of transformation. Embrace the journey of the Phoenix, using the insights gained from the flames of adversity to illuminate your path forward. Your resilience, courage, and spirit shine as beacons of hope for both yourself and others on similar journeys.

Remember, you're never alone on this path. Reach out, seek support, and always hold onto the belief that brighter days await. The Phoenix's rise is a testament to the power of rebirth and resurgence. Embrace your Phoenix journey, knowing that your wings, though scorched, possess the strength to soar once more.

5

THE ASHES

ACKNOWLEDGING AND ACCEPTING THE IMPACT

Acknowledging the reality of one's experience is a cornerstone in the journey of healing. In my decades of practice, I've often observed that one of the most challenging steps for survivors of narcissistic abuse is the very act of recognition and acceptance of what they've undergone. This reluctance isn't due to ignorance or naivety. Rather, it's often tied to the insidious nature of narcissistic abuse and the intense emotions it evokes.

Narcissistic abuse, unlike some forms of physical violence, often operates in the shadows. Its covert nature can be so subtle that many victims find themselves ensnared before they even recognize the signs. The narcissist's actions are often cloaked in a façade of love, concern, or simply the routine dynamics of a relationship. Over time, the very reality the victim resides in can become warped, leading them to question their perceptions, beliefs, and even their sanity.

Beyond the covert nature of the abuse, fear plays a significant role in the reluctance to acknowledge it. Fear of retaliation from the narcissist, fear of judgment from others, and even the fear of confronting the depth of the pain can create an invisible barrier that holds victims back from accepting their reality.

Moreover, the very idea of acknowledging such profound betrayal, especially if it comes from someone dearly loved or trusted, can be overwhelming. It requires not just understanding but also immense emotional strength to come to terms with the reality that someone they cherished could inflict such harm.

If you find yourself resonating with these sentiments, please know that you are not alone. Your feelings, no matter how conflicting or overwhelming they might seem, are valid. Acceptance of narcissistic abuse is not about finding blame in yourself or dwelling on the past, but about understanding the magnitude of your experience. It's about laying the groundwork for healing.

Imagine, for a moment, a Phoenix—majestic and strong. Before its rebirth, it must first recognize and embrace its ashes. Similarly, acknowledging the depths of the pain you've experienced is akin to embracing those ashes, laying the foundation for your impending transformation and resurgence.

In my personal journey, grappling with the realization that I was in a relationship with a malignant narcissist was a daunting task. I understand the depth of courage it takes to face this truth. And while the path is undeni-ably challenging, let me assure you that recognizing the reality is a monumental stride towards reclaiming your life and spirit.

We will now delve deeper into the emotional and psychological landscapes carved out by such abuse. Through understanding, acceptance, and resilience, you will find the strength to rise again, just as the Phoenix does—stronger, brighter, and more powerful than before.

One of the profound consequences of narcissistic abuse is the storm of emotions it stirs within its victims. While each individual's experience is unique, many survivors report overlapping feelings that can often be intense, conflicting, and deeply unsettling. Navigating this turbulent emotional landscape is a critical step in the healing journey.

1. Confusion: At the onset, many survivors grapple with a profound sense of confusion. The duality of a narcissist—where moments of affection are juxtaposed with instances of cruelty—can leave one questioning the nature of the relationship. Was it all genuine? Were there genuine moments of love? Or was it all an illusion? This constant questioning can be mentally exhausting, creating a fog of uncertainty around memo-ries and experiences.

2. Guilt: Coupled with confusion, many victims feel an unwarranted sense of guilt. The narcissist, with their knack for manipulation, often succeeds in shifting the blame for the relationship's toxic dynamics onto the victim. This can lead to feelings of self-blame and a lingering sense that one might have done something different to prevent the abuse.

3. Shame: Beyond guilt, there's a pervasive sense of shame. Many survivors express feeling embarrassed about having been manipulated or not recognizing the signs sooner. Remember, shame thrives in silence. Speaking about your experience, whether in therapy or with trusted individuals, can be a potent antidote.

4. Fear: Fear, a constant companion for many during the relationship, often lingers long after it has ended. Fear of the narcissist's retaliation, fear of future relationships, or simply fear of being vulnerable again can be paralyzing.

5. Anger: As the fog of confusion starts to lift, many victims feel a surge of anger. Anger at the narcissist for the betrayal, anger at themselves for not recognizing the signs, and sometimes, anger at those who might have witnessed the abuse but remained silent. While anger is a natural and valid response, it's essential to channel it constructively, using it as a catalyst for healing rather than allowing it to consume you.

6. Grief: In the aftermath of acknowledging the abuse, a profound sense of grief often emerges. This is a mourning process not just for the relationship but also for the loss of trust, time, and the emotional investment made. It's a grief for the dreams that were built and the future that was envisioned.

While this spectrum of emotions might seem overwhelming, it's crucial to understand that each emotion, no matter how painful, is a step towards healing. Just as a wound needs to be cleaned before it can heal, these emotions need to be fully felt, understood, and processed.

In my own journey, the weight of these emotions often felt unbearable. But with time, patience, and the right support, I learned that each emotion was a layer, revealing a deeper understanding of myself and the experience I had undergone. And just as a Phoenix needs to embrace its entire being—both its fiery spirit and its ashes—you too must embrace the entirety of your emotions to truly soar again.

In the quiet spaces of introspection, during meditation, or in the comforting embrace of nature, allow yourself to feel. Give yourself permission to grieve, to be angry, to confront your fears. Because within these emotions lies not just the scars of the past, but the seeds of your resurgence and rebirth.

Narcissistic abuse does not merely scratch the surface; it pierces deep, affecting the very core of an individual's psychological well-being. Over my years of practice, I've had countless conversations with survivors, and the patterns of psychological distress they experience are consistent and heartbreaking. Backed by research and illustrated through stories from my practice, here's a dive into the profound psychological impacts of narcissistic abuse:

1. Eroded Self-Esteem: One of the hallmarks of narcissistic abuse is the systematic dismantling of the victim's self-worth. Survivors often share how they were once confident, only to be reduced to shadows of their former selves. Over time, the constant belittling, criticism, and emotional manipulation chip away at the victim's sense of value.

In my therapy room, I remember a talented musician who had stopped playing her instrument because her narcissistic partner convinced her she "had no real talent." This belief was so deeply ingrained that even years after leaving the abusive relationship, she hesitated to touch the keys.

2. Difficulty Trusting Others: The betrayal experienced in a relationship with a narcissist can lead to profound trust issues. If the person who professed love could cause such harm, then who can be trusted? This skepticism can bleed into other relationships, creating barriers to intimacy and genuine connection.

A patient once shared with me how she'd set up "tests" for new potential partners, attempting to determine their sincerity. The fear of being manipulated again was so intense that she'd inadvertently push away genuine individuals trying to get close.

3. Tendency to Self-Isolate: Often, victims of narcissistic abuse begin to withdraw from their social circles. The isolation might start subtly—missing an occasional gathering due to the narcissist's demands. But over time, the victim may distance themselves, either out of shame or because they've been conditioned to believe that their loved ones are "against them."

I recall a gentleman who had been so isolated by his narcissistic wife that he hadn't seen his family in years. He believed they'd abandoned him, only to later discover a trail of unanswered messages, calls, and attempts to reach out.

4. Hyper-Vigilance: Living with a narcissist often means walking on eggshells. Over time, this heightened state of alertness can become the norm. Survivors may find themselves constantly scanning their environment for potential threats, a state of being which can be exhausting and anxiety-inducing.

One woman described it as "always waiting for the other shoe to drop." Even in peaceful settings, she was braced

for chaos, so accustomed to it from her previous rela-
tionship.

5. Doubting One's Reality: Constant gaslighting —a manipulative tactic where the abuser denies or twists the victim's reality—can lead survivors to doubt their perceptions and memories. This cognitive dissonance can be debilitating, causing the victim to question their sanity.

An anecdote that stands out is of a young man who kept a secret journal. He'd note down events and conversations because his narcissistic partner often denied things that had clearly happened. This journal became his anchor to reality.

The ramifications of narcissistic abuse are vast and deeply ingrained. Yet, understanding them is crucial. By identifying and acknowledging these impacts, survivors take a significant step towards addressing them. Like a Phoenix meticulously preening its wings, attending to each feather, acknowledging each scar, and preparing for its ascent, survivors too can address each psychological wound, nurturing themselves back to wholeness and strength.

In the ever-evolving journey of healing, acceptance stands as a pivotal cornerstone. To many, this word carries an undeserved weight, mistaken for resignation or even endorsement of the abuser's behavior. But true acceptance is far removed from these misconceptions. It is not about condoning or justifying any wrong done, but rather about confronting the reality of one's experience and the emotions that arise from it.

Let's delve into the true essence of acceptance.

Understanding Acceptance: At its heart, acceptance is the recognition of one's lived experiences. It's giving oneself permission to say, "This happened to me. It hurt me. And it's okay to admit that pain." This seemingly simple acknowledgment is an act of tremendous courage. By seeing the situation for what it truly was, devoid of any self-blame or distortion, one lays the foundation for authentic healing.

Acceptance vs. Condoning: There's a profound difference between understanding something and endorsing it. Accepting that you were subjected to narcissistic abuse doesn't mean you believe the actions were right or deserved. It simply means that you are choosing to see the situation with clear eyes, free from denial or minimization. By doing so, you reclaim your narrative, ensuring that it is defined by your truth and not the narcissist's manipulations.

The Phoenix and Its Ashes: Envision the Phoenix, that radiant mythical creature, reborn from the ashes of its predecessor. The ashes are not just remnants of its past but the very essence from which its future emerges. Similarly, acceptance can be seen as the ashes of our experiences. By acknowledging and understanding the depths of these ashes, we create the foundation from which we can rise again, renewed and empowered. Denying or avoiding the reality of our past keeps us bound to it, but embracing it gives us the momentum to soar to new heights.

The Healing Power of Acceptance: By accepting your journey and the wounds incurred along the way, you open the door to transformation. Acceptance paves the way for compassion, forgiveness (of oneself), and ultimately, growth. It's akin to clearing the debris after a storm, making space for new, robust structures to be built.

In my own journey, there was a pivotal moment when I had to face the reality of my experiences, no matter how painful they were. It was only when I fully embraced this acceptance that the true healing began, allowing me to rise, Phoenix-like, from the ashes of my past, stronger and more resolute in my purpose.

As you traverse your own path, remember that acceptance is not a destination but a continuous process. Each day, as you acknowledge your feelings, experiences, and truths, you feed the flames of your own rebirth, preparing for the magnificent ascent that awaits.

Embarking on a journey of introspection is akin to navigating a vast forest. Some paths are sunlit and clear, while others are shadowy and entwined with underbrush. But each step, even the challenging ones, leads to greater understanding and clarity. To help you on this path, I offer a series of reflective prompts. These are gentle nudges to encourage deeper exploration of your feelings, emotions, and experiences. They serve as catalysts for self-discovery and acceptance.

As you engage with each prompt, remember that there is no 'right' or 'wrong' response. Your thoughts and feelings are valid and unique to your journey. Allow yourself the grace to write freely, without judgment or constraint.

1. Recognition: Describe a moment when you first recognized that something was amiss in your relationship. What signs or feelings led you to this realization?

2. Feelings Spectrum: List down the emotions you've felt during and after the abuse. For each emotion, describe a specific instance that elicited that feeling. This exercise helps in identifying patterns and triggers.

3. Lost and Found: Think of a part of yourself or a personal interest that got overshadowed or lost during the relationship. How can you reclaim or rediscover that aspect of yourself?

4. The Mirror: Narcissistic abuse often distorts our self-perception. Write a compassionate letter to yourself, highlighting your strengths, qualities, and achievements. Read it whenever self-doubt creeps in.

5. Trust Inventory: Reflect on how your ability to trust—both yourself and others—has been impacted. What steps can you envision to rebuild that trust over time?

6. Phoenix Visualization: Imagine yourself as the Phoenix, rising from the ashes. What do those ashes represent in your life? And as you rise, what changes, transformations, or newfound strengths do you see in yourself?

7. Acceptance and Healing: What does acceptance look like to you? Describe a moment when you felt a glimmer of acceptance, no matter how fleeting.

8. Dreams and Desires: List down things you wish to achieve or experience, both in your personal growth and external life, in the post-recovery phase. This could include skills, travel, relationships, or any personal milestones.

Using these prompts as a starting point, let your pen flow, allowing it to draw out the intricacies of your emotions and experiences. Over time, you'll find that these reflective exercises become sacred moments of self-connection, fostering a deeper understanding and acceptance of your journey. Remember, just as the Phoenix rises anew each time, every reflection offers a chance for rebirth and transformation.

Recognizing the nuanced shades of narcissistic abuse, understanding its profound emotional and psychological impact, and then journeying towards acceptance is no small feat. Each step requires courage, resilience, and an unwavering commitment to oneself.

Many victims find themselves tangled in a web of denial and confusion, a natural defense mechanism against the covert and insidious nature of this form of abuse. But as we've learned, facing this reality, even when painful, is essential for healing. By acknowledging the abuse and embracing the whirlwind of emotions it elicits, we lay the foundation for deeper understanding and healing.

The psychological repercussions of narcissistic abuse can be profound, affecting our self-worth, our ability to trust, and our connection to the world around us. Yet, through introspection, guided reflection, and therapeutic intervention, healing is not just a possibility but a certainty.

Acceptance is the cornerstone of this healing journey. Like the Phoenix, our rebirth is only possible when we acknowledge the ashes of our past. Accepting doesn't mean condoning or forgetting. It means understanding, giving oneself permission to grieve, and eventually finding the strength to move forward.

In the chapters to come, we will delve deeper into the transformative process of rising from the ashes. We'll explore the tools and techniques to rebuild oneself, foster healthier relationships, and reclaim the life you deserve. The journey ahead will be challenging, yet immensely rewarding. Just remember, like the Phoenix, you are destined to rise, to soar, and to shine once more.

As we venture further into this path of recovery, I'll be with you every step of the way, offering insights, guidance, and encouragement. The strength that has carried you this far will propel you even further. Embrace the journey, for it is in traversing these challenges that we find our true selves, emerging stronger, wiser, and more resilient than ever before.

6

SPARKS OF CHANGE

PREPARING FOR THE JOURNEY AHEAD

In the heart of a dense, dark forest, imagine a single spark. It may seem inconsequential amid the overwhelming darkness, but given the right conditions, that tiny spark can ignite a transformative fire, illuminating the way forward and clearing the path for new growth. Similarly, in the maze of pain and confusion that often characterizes the aftermath of narcissistic abuse, the decision to change, to rise above, can be that vital spark.

The decision to embark on a healing journey, to reclaim one's life, is profoundly powerful. Yet, it's essential to acknowledge that arriving at this decision is seldom straightforward. For many, it's a path laden with doubts, fears, and potential resistance.

Imagine Sarah, a former client of mine. Having been in a relationship with a narcissistic partner for several years, she was entangled in a web of manipulation, guilt, and self-blame. Every time she mustered the courage to consider a life free from abuse, nagging doubts held her back: "What if I'm overreacting?" "Maybe it's all in my head?" "What if I can't handle life without him?" Such doubts are common and are often fueled by the gaslighting and emotional manipulation characteristic of narcissistic abuse.

Moreover, the decision to change is often accompanied by a spectrum of fears. The fear of the unknown, fear of retaliation from the narcissist, fear of judgment from others, or even the fear of truly facing the depth of the trauma. As someone who has walked this path, I remember the nights spent wrestling with these very anxieties, wondering if the weight of the past would forever chain me to a life of pain.

Yet, amidst these challenges, there's a resilient force within each survivor, a yearning for peace, love, and genuine happiness. Think of it as the Phoenix within, waiting for its chance to rise from the ashes. The moment we decide to heed this inner call, we light the spark that can set our transformation in motion.

Drawing from my own experience and witnessing countless survivors in my practice, I've seen how this decisive moment—this profound choice—can lead to a transformative journey. Alex, another individual I had the privilege of guiding, once told me, "The day I decided to heal was the day I took back control of my life." And he was right. The journey ahead might be long and tumultuous, but the power of that initial decision serves as a guiding light, illuminating the path towards healing and self-discovery.

In embracing this decision, you're not just choosing to move away from pain; you're moving towards hope, self-love, and a brighter, more authentic future. Remember, every great journey begins with a single, determined step. And acknowledging the need for change, for healing, is that monumental first step.

Just as a traveler prepares for a long expedition by gathering supplies and mapping out a route, survivors of narcissistic abuse must prepare mentally for their healing journey. This preparation is paramount, as the path to recovery can be winding and at times steep, with its set of challenges and unexpected turns. But with the right mindset and tools, one can navigate this journey with resilience and grace.

1. Cultivating a Positive Mindset:

It's often said that our mind is the most potent tool we possess. A positive mindset isn't about ignoring pain or glossing over trauma; rather, it's about holding onto the belief that healing is possible and recognizing your innate strength.

Tip: Begin each day with a positive affirmation. Statements like, "I am worthy of healing," "I possess the strength to overcome this," or "Each day, I grow stronger and more resilient," can serve as daily reminders of your power and determination.

2. Managing Expectations:

Healing is not linear. There will be days when you feel like you're making great strides, and others when it seems like you've taken a few steps back. It's essential to set realistic expectations and understand that healing is a process, with its ebbs and flows.

Tip: Visualize your healing journey as a mountain trek. While reaching the summit is the ultimate goal, there will be valleys, plateaus, and even occasional descents. Celebrate every step, and remember that even on the challenging days, you're still making progress.

3. Embracing the Ups and Downs:

It's natural to have fluctuations in mood and emotion during the healing process. Some days will be harder than others. Embrace these ups and downs as part and parcel of your journey, understanding that every challenge faced is an opportunity for growth.

Tip: Create a "healing journal" where you document your emotions, challenges, and victories. Over time, this can serve as a testament to your resilience and growth, reminding you of how far you've come.

4. Staying Mentally Engaged:

Keeping the mind active and engaged can serve as a form of therapy. Whether it's through reading, learning a new skill, or indulging in a hobby like meditation or yoga (which I personally find very grounding), these activities can provide a welcome distraction and offer new perspectives.

Tip: Dedicate a few minutes each day to an activity you love or are curious about. It could be reading a chapter from a motivational book, practicing deep breathing exercises, or even solving puzzles. The idea is to keep the mind active and focused.

5. Seeking Support:

You don't have to walk this path alone. Whether it's through therapy, support groups, or connecting with trusted friends and family, surrounding yourself with a support system can bolster your mental preparedness.

Tip: Consider joining a support group, either in-person or online, where you can share your experiences, gain insights from others on a similar journey, and celebrate mutual milestones.

In essence, mental preparation is about equipping yourself with the tools and mindset needed to navigate the healing journey. While challenges are inevitable, with the right strategies and a resilient mindset, you can continue moving forward, inching closer to your summit of healing and self-discovery. Remember, just like the Phoenix that soars from the ashes, with each challenge faced, you too can rise stronger and more radiant.

In the aftermath of narcissistic abuse, the landscape of one's soul can feel barren, scorched by the fiery trials faced. However, just as a phoenix requires nourishment to rise from the ashes, survivors too need to prioritize self-care to rejuvenate and heal. Often mistaken as a luxurious indulgence, self-care is, in reality, a fundamental cornerstone of recovery. It's the conscious act of refueling our body, mind, and spirit, ensuring that we're equipped with the strength and vitality required for the journey ahead.

Physical Self-care: The Body's Resilience

The physical aftermath of prolonged stress and trauma can be quite profound. A body under duress may manifest signs of fatigue, sleep disturbances, or even weakened immunity. Prioritizing physical health becomes essential not just for overall well-being but as a way to fortify oneself against these potential ailments.

1. Healthy Diet: The foods we consume can have a profound effect on our mood and energy levels. Prioritize a balanced diet, rich in whole foods, lean proteins, healthy fats, and a variety of fruits and vegetables. Remember that what we feed our body also nourishes our mind and spirit.

Tip: Incorporate mood-boosting foods like fatty fish (rich in Omega-3s), dark chocolate (in moderation), and green tea, which have been shown to have positive effects on mental well-being.

2. Exercise: Physical activity releases endorphins, the body's natural mood boosters. Whether it's a brisk walk in nature, a rejuvenating yoga session (a personal favorite of mine), or a more intense workout, find an activity that resonates with you and make it a part of your routine.

Tip: If you're new to exercise, start with short, manageable sessions and gradually build up. Celebrate every accomplishment, no matter how small.

3. Sleep: A rested body is a resilient body. Prioritize good sleep hygiene by setting a regular sleep schedule, creating a calm bedtime routine, and ensuring your sleeping environment is conducive to rest.

Tip: Consider incorporating relaxation techniques like deep breathing or guided meditations to aid in sleep. I've often found that a few minutes of meditation before bed can make a world of difference.

Emotional Self-care: Tending to the Soul

While physical health is crucial, the emotional scars left behind by narcissistic abuse require equal, if not more, attention.

1. Mindfulness: The practice of being present can serve as an anchor during tumultuous times. Whether it's through meditation, deep breathing exercises, or simply being attuned to the present moment, mindfulness can offer a reprieve from intrusive thoughts and anxieties.

Tip: If you're new to mindfulness, start with short daily practices. There are numerous apps and online resources that offer guided sessions tailored for beginners.

2. Therapy: Engaging in therapy with a professional experienced in narcissistic abuse can offer insights, coping strategies, and a safe space to process your emotions.

Tip: If you're unsure where to start, consider seeking recommendations or researching therapists who specialize in narcissistic abuse recovery.

3. Support Groups: Connecting with others who've walked a similar path can offer solace, under-standing, and camaraderie. Support groups, whether in-person or online, provide a platform to share experi-ences, gain insights, and celebrate mutual milestones.

Tip: When joining a support group, ensure it's a safe and moderated environment that aligns with your healing goals.

In conclusion, self-care is not just a means of recovery but a declaration of self-worth. It's an affirmation that you value yourself, recognizing the importance of replenishing the soul, and ensuring you're at your best for the journey ahead. Just as the Phoenix requires the right conditions to rise gloriously from the ashes, by embracing self-care, you too are setting the stage for your radiant ascent.

As we nurture our minds and bodies through the various self-care practices, we begin to rebuild our sense of worth and rediscover our inner strengths. Just as a tree needs rich soil to anchor its roots and draw nutrients, our souls require a supportive environment to truly flourish. Part of creating this nurturing landscape involves not just what we give to ourselves but also what we prevent from depleting us. After feeding our spirits with self-care, it becomes crucial to shield them from external forces that might drain our renewed energy. This protective barrier is achieved by setting and maintaining firm boundaries. Let's delve into understanding these boundaries and how they fortify our journey to healing.

Boundaries, in essence, are invisible lines we draw to protect our energy, self-worth, and well-being. Think of them as the protective walls around the sanctuary of your soul, delineating where you end and others begin. In the context of narcissistic abuse, boundaries become indispensable shields against further harm, ensuring that we don't find ourselves ensnared in the same damaging dynamics again.

Why Boundaries Are Essential:

1. Protection from Further Abuse: Narcissists often exploit porous boundaries, taking advantage of the generous, empathetic nature of their targets. Setting firm boundaries ensures that the avenues for manipulation are closed.

2. Preserving Emotional Health: When boundaries are clear and upheld, it becomes easier to differentiate between one's emotions and the external pressures or projections of others, resulting in less emotional turmoil.

3. Promoting Self-Respect: Boundaries are a testament to self-worth. By enforcing them, you're affirming that your needs, emotions, and well-being are valid and deserving of respect.

Practical Tips for Setting and Enforcing Boundaries:

1. Self-awareness: Before setting boundaries, it's essential to understand your own needs, desires, and limits. Ask yourself: What makes you uncomfortable? What behaviors will you not tolerate? This introspection forms the foundation of effective boundary-setting.

2. Clear Communication: Articulate your boundaries in a clear, concise manner. For instance, if a narcissistic ex-partner attempts to reconnect, you might say, "For my well-being, I've chosen not to have any contact with you. Please respect my wishes."

3. Stay Firm: Narcissists might test or push against your boundaries. It's crucial to remain steadfast. For example, if you've decided to limit contact to only essential matters, and they try to engage in trivial conversations, remind them of the boundary and disengage.

4. Seek Support: Setting boundaries, especially with a narcissist, can be challenging. Surround yourself with supportive friends or family, or consider joining a support group. Their encouragement can bolster your resolve.

5. Avoid JADE (Justify, Argue, Defend, Explain): When enforcing boundaries, it's essential to avoid getting dragged into long-winded explanations or justifications. Remember, boundaries are a statement of your needs, not a debate.

6. Practice Self-Care: As discussed in the previous section, nurturing yourself can fortify your emotional strength, making it easier to set and maintain boundaries.

7. Reassess and Adjust: As you grow and evolve on your healing journey, your boundaries might shift. Periodically reassess them to ensure they align with your current needs and feelings.

Examples of Setting Boundaries:

- **Physical Boundaries:** If a narcissistic family member has a habit of showing up unannounced, communicate that they need to call and schedule a visit beforehand.

- **Emotional Boundaries:** If a friend frequently dumps their emotional baggage on you without regard for your feelings, let them know that you need conversations to be reciprocal and supportive.
- **Digital Boundaries:** If you find that interacting with a narcissistic individual on social media is harmful, consider muting, blocking, or unfriending them.

Setting boundaries is not about being confrontational or unkind; it's about safeguarding your well-being. As you journey towards healing, view these boundaries as the nurturing soil in which your Phoenix can safely rest, rejuvenate, and eventually, rise. Boundaries don't imprison us; rather, they liberate us, allowing our spirits to soar unencumbered.

The journey of healing and recovery is deeply personal, and introspection plays a pivotal role in understanding and navigating our path. To aid in this self-exploration, I've designed a series of reflective prompts and questions. Engaging with these can help you assess where you are, where you want to be, and the tools you need to get there.

1. Readiness for Change:

- When you think about your healing journey, what emotions arise? Are they mainly positive, negative, or a mix of both?
- Recall a moment when you felt empowered to make a change in your life. What triggered that feeling, and how can you draw on it now?
- What are the primary obstacles or fears holding you back from fully committing to your recovery journey? How might you address or overcome them?

2. Self-Care Strategies:

- List down five activities that genuinely make you feel rejuvenated and centered. How can you incorporate these into your daily or weekly routine?
- How do you currently respond to stress or emotional turmoil? How might self-care reshape these reactions?
- Reflect on your support system. Are there specific people or groups that you can rely on during tough times? If not, how might you seek out these supportive networks?

3. Boundary-Setting Needs:

- Think of a recent situation where you felt your boundaries were crossed. What feelings arose, and how did you respond?

- What boundaries do you feel are most crucial for your emotional well-being? Are there any specific areas where you often feel violated or disrespected?
- Visualize a scenario where you successfully set and maintain a boundary. How does it make you feel? What strategies did you use, and how can you implement them in real-life situations?

As you ponder these questions, remember that your answers might evolve over time. The healing journey, much like the rise of the Phoenix, is marked by cycles of introspection, growth, and renewal. Embrace each stage with compassion and the understanding that you are making progress, no matter how slow or incremental it might seem.

As we bring this chapter to a close, it's essential to reflect on the keystones we've laid down for your healing journey. First and foremost, remember that the *decision to change* stands as the cornerstone, the foundational spark that ignites the transformative process. Your conscious choice to embark on this path, despite the challenges, fears, and potential resistance, is a testament to your strength and resilience.

Mental preparation cannot be overstated. Like a diligent gardener tending to the soil before planting, nurturing a positive mindset, setting realistic expectations, and embracing the inevitable highs and lows of recovery ensures that the seeds of healing can take root and flourish.

Self-care is the sustenance on this journey. Both physical and emotional self-care acts as the life-giving water and sunlight, helping you grow, replenish, and regain the strength that might have been sapped away. It isn't just a luxury—it's a crucial aspect of your recovery, ensuring you have the vitality and well-being to continue forward.

Lastly, the art of **setting boundaries** is akin to erecting protective fences around a budding plant, ensuring that it is shielded from any external harm. In the context of your healing, boundaries safeguard your emotional and mental health, fortifying you against any potential intrusions or setbacks.

As we move on to our next chapter, we will delve deeper into the art of rebuilding, much like the Phoenix rising from its ashes, crafting a life of empowerment, joy, and purpose. Always remember, the journey of a thousand miles begins with a single step. With each day, with each reflection, and with each boundary set, you're not just moving forward; you're soaring. The sky is limitless, and so is your potential. Embrace the journey with hope, and always know that you are not alone in this.

RISING FROM THE ASHES

BREAKING FREE FROM NARCISSISTIC ABUSE

It was a crisp autumn morning, a kind that fills the air with a promise of change. I found myself in a quaint coffee shop, wrapping my hands around a warm mug, when an old friend from college, Laura, walked in. She looked different; the spark in her eyes I remembered was dimmed, and her posture seemed weighed down. We settled into a corner, and as the conversation flowed, Laura unveiled her ongoing relationship with someone I soon realized was a narcissist. She described a cycle of emotional upheavals, manipulations, and a deep-rooted feeling of being trapped. I saw in Laura a reflection of my younger self, lost in the maze of a toxic relationship.

As I listened to Laura, memories flooded back: the similar entrapment I felt, the desire to escape yet being anchored by a mix of fear, loyalty, and hope that things would change. But, like Laura, I reached a turning point. A realization that for the Phoenix to rise, it must first free itself from the confining ashes. For Laura, and many others like us, disengaging from a narcissist is that path to liberation.

Breaking free from the grips of a narcissistic relationship is not just a step towards healing but a monumental leap towards self-discovery and personal growth. At the heart of narcissistic abuse lies a tangled web of manipulation, gaslighting, and emotional exploitation. Over time, these insidious patterns can erode one's sense of self, distort realities, and instill a profound sense of entrapment.

As a seasoned psychologist and someone who has personally navigated the turbulent waters of a relationship with a malignant narcissist, I can attest to the profound need for disengagement. Breaking free from the grips of a narcissistic relationship is not only a step towards healing but a leap towards self-liberation and growth.

At the heart of narcissistic abuse lies a web of manipulation, gaslighting, and emotional exploitation. Over time, these patterns can erode one's sense of self, distort realities, and foster a profound sense of entrapment. Just like the Phoenix, there comes a point when you realize that to truly rise and embrace your potential, you must first free yourself from the ashes that weigh you down. And in the context of narcissistic abuse, this often means disengaging from the narcissist.

However, as with any significant change, the process is rarely straightforward. The journey towards disengagement may be fraught with challenges. Narcissists, fearing a loss of control, might escalate their tactics, ranging from emotional blackmail to overt threats. There might be shared responsibilities, like children or financial entanglements, complicating the decision. Social circles, familial ties, and even workplace dynamics can present added layers of complexity.

Furthermore, within oneself, there might be a tumult of emotions: guilt for "abandoning" the relationship, fear of the unknown, or doubts about one's capacity to thrive independently. These feelings are natural and valid. The decision to disengage is monumental, and it's not unusual for the path to be peppered with obstacles both external and internal.

Yet, it is vital to remember that true healing, growth, and transformation often require us to step out of our comfort zones and confront these challenges head-on. By understanding the necessity of disengagement and arming ourselves with knowledge, support, and resilience, we can navigate this complex terrain and set the stage for a life that is no longer overshadowed by narcissistic abuse.

Crafting an effective escape plan from a narcissistic relationship requires thoughtful consideration and meticulous planning. When ensnared in such relationships, a well-structured plan becomes the beacon of light guiding one towards freedom. Let's dive deep into the components of this blueprint.

1. Financial Independence:

- Assessment: Begin by understanding your current financial situation. Catalog your assets, liabilities, income, and monthly expenses.
- Separation: Open a new bank account in your name alone. Consider using a different bank than the one where shared accounts may be held.
- Budgeting: Create a financial plan for after the separation. Anticipate and factor in initial costs such as housing deposits, legal fees, or therapy.

2. Housing Considerations:

- Research: Investigate affordable and safe housing options. Local women's shelters or organizations may have resources or recommendations.
- Confidentiality: When looking for new housing, ensure your searches and inquiries remain private, using private browsing modes and avoiding shared devices.
- Safety Measures: Once you've secured a place, consider changing locks, installing

security systems, and informing trusted neighbors about your situation.

3. Social Support:

- Build a Support Team: Surrounding yourself with empathetic friends and family can be instrumental. Brief them about your plan so they can be there for you during and after the transition.
- Avoid Common Acquaintances: It might be prudent to distance yourself from mutual friends or acquaintances who might unintentionally relay information back to the narcissist.
- Support Groups: Seek out local or online support groups. Shared experiences can provide understanding and strength.

4. Mental Health Resources:

- Therapy: Engage in individual therapy with professionals familiar with narcissistic abuse. This provides tailored strategies and coping mechanisms.
- Emergency Helplines: Have the number of emergency helplines on hand. These can offer immediate guidance during crisis moments.

- Mindfulness and Meditation: My own journey of healing was significantly enhanced by practices like yoga and meditation. They can anchor and calm your mind amidst the storm.

Throughout this process, it's paramount to prioritize safety and confidentiality. Always remember, the narcissist might escalate their behavior when sensing a loss of control. Thus, ensuring your plan remains covert is essential. Consider using password protection on your devices, clearing browser histories, or even using public computers for sensitive searches.

In every step of this blueprint, visualize your end goal: a life free from the heavy chains of narcissism, a life where you rise, strong and rejuvenated.

Taking flight from a narcissistic relationship often goes beyond emotional and psychological preparation. The legal landscape can be intricate, requiring both knowledge and strategy, much like a Phoenix needing to understand the winds before it can soar. Here are some key legal considerations you should be aware of:

1. Divorce Laws:

- Grounds for Divorce: Depending on your jurisdiction, there might be specific criteria required to file for divorce. While some

places offer no-fault divorces, others might
require proof of wrongdoing.

- Property and Asset Division: The division of
property, assets, and debts can vary. Some
jurisdictions split marital assets equally, while
others look at factors such as each party's
earning capacity and contributions to the
marriage.
- Alimony: Depending on the circumstances,
you might be eligible for spousal support, or
conversely, might have to provide it.

2. Child Custody and Support:

- Types of Custody: Custody can be joint or
sole, and it encompasses both physical
custody (where the child resides) and legal
custody (decision-making power about the
child's upbringing).
- Best Interests of the Child: Courts typically
prioritize the child's best interests. Factors can
include the child's age, the parent's mental
and physical health, and any history of
domestic violence.
- Child Support: Regardless of custody
arrangements, non-custodial parents might be
required to provide financial support. This is
typically calculated based on income,
childcare costs, and other factors.

RISING FROM THE ASHES

3. Restraining and Protective Orders:

- Immediate Safety: If you fear for your safety
  or that of your children, seek a restraining
  order. This legally prohibits the narcissist
  from approaching or contacting you.
- Temporary vs. Permanent Orders: Initially,
  you might be granted a temporary order.
  After a court hearing, this can be extended
  into a permanent one, which lasts longer.
- Violation Consequences: Breaching these
  orders can lead to legal consequences for the
  narcissist, from fines to imprisonment.

While these points provide an overview, it's crucial to
remember that laws and regulations vary depending on
your jurisdiction. I cannot stress enough the importance of seeking professional legal counsel. An experienced attorney can offer guidance tailored to your
specific situation, helping you navigate the maze of
laws and ensuring that your rights are protected.

In my own journey, understanding my legal rights was
both empowering and liberating. It provided a strong
foundation upon which I could rebuild my life. I urge
you to take this step, not just as a legal necessity, but as
a pathway to reclaiming your autonomy and freedom.
Remember, the flight of the Phoenix begins with a
single upward beat of its wings.

Navigating the social maze after disentangling oneself from a narcissist can be reminiscent of the Phoenix's rebirth – emerging from ashes, its flight path uncertain, yet filled with newfound clarity and hope. Here are some vital considerations and strategies for the social phase of your journey:

1. Managing Shared Friendships:

- Open Communication: Speak to close friends about your decision to part ways with the narcissist. You don't need to give intricate details, but it's essential to communicate your perspective.
- Avoiding Triangulation: Narcissists often use triangulation, manipulating two people against each other. If a friend seems to be conveying the narcissist's views or messages, set boundaries or reconsider the value of that friendship.
- Deciding What's Best for You: Some friends may choose neutrality, while others might pick a side. It's essential to surround yourself with supportive and understanding friends during this transition. Remember, it's okay to outgrow relationships that no longer align with your well-being.

2. Handling Smear Campaigns and Retaliation:

- Stay Grounded: Narcissists might start smear campaigns to tarnish your reputation. Maintain your dignity by not engaging in mud-slinging. Your actions and character will speak louder than any rumors.
- Seek Support: Connecting with support groups, therapists, or close friends who understand narcissistic behavior can provide validation and help counteract the isolation that might result from smearing.
- Protect Yourself: If the narcissist's retaliation goes beyond words and impacts your safety, consider seeking legal protection.

3. Building New, Healthy Social Connections:

- Pursue Interests: Engage in activities you love, be it yoga, reading, or hiking. These can be pathways to meet like-minded individuals who share your passions.
- Seek Support Groups: Organizations and groups dedicated to helping survivors of narcissistic abuse can be invaluable. They offer a space of understanding and shared experiences, providing both solace and strategies for healing.
- Learn and Grow: Use this period as an opportunity to understand and establish your

relationship boundaries better. Empower
yourself with knowledge and, over time, trust
your instincts as you form new connections.

In my own experience, while there were moments of
loneliness, they were juxtaposed with times of
profound self-discovery and connections with
genuinely empathetic souls. The journey, like that of
the Phoenix, is cyclical – periods of solitude and reflection followed by soaring towards new horizons.
Embrace every stage, for each one is a stepping stone
towards a more authentic and fulfilling life.

The path to disengagement from a narcissist is paved
with introspection and deliberate choices. By setting
aside dedicated moments for reflection, you'll harness
the insights needed to fly freely. Here are some reflective questions and journal prompts to guide you:

1. Assessing the Relationship

- What emotions or incidents prompted you to
  consider disengaging from the narcissist?
- List down three pivotal moments in the
  relationship that were turning points for you.

2. Your Support System

- Who in your life truly understands your situation and provides genuine support? How have they shown their support in the past?
- How can you further strengthen or expand your support circle during this transition?

3. Crafting an Escape Blueprint

- What are the primary resources (financial, emotional, physical) you'll need to establish independence from the narcissist?
- Outline a timeline or plan for securing these resources. What are the potential obstacles, and how can you navigate them?

4. Legal and Social Anticipations

- If you were to describe your ideal post-separation scenario, what would it look like?
- How can you prepare for potential legal battles or smear campaigns? What resources or allies might you need?

5. Rebuilding and Renewal

- What boundaries will you set in future relationships to prevent a recurrence of past patterns?

- Envision a life free from the narcissist's influence. What activities or aspirations would you pursue? How would your daily life look?

6. Finding Strength in Reflection

- Recall a moment when you felt particularly resilient or empowered. What led to that feeling?
- How can you regularly tap into that strength and determination as you journey towards liberation?

I encourage you to visit these prompts regularly, updating your responses as your circumstances evolve and new insights emerge. As you do, remember that, like the Phoenix, your transformative journey is a testament to your indomitable spirit and the brighter horizons that await.

The journey to liberation from the grip of narcissistic abuse requires both courage and deliberate action. In this chapter, we've delved deep into the necessity of disengagement, emphasizing its pivotal role in healing and personal growth. Crafting an escape blueprint demands careful planning, spanning financial independence, securing housing, leaning on social support, and tapping into mental health resources. Additionally, understanding the legal landscape, from divorce intricacies to child custody and restraining orders, is essential. It safeguards you from potential pitfalls and fortifies your path to freedom.

Equally crucial is the navigation of the social maze. As you disentangle from the narcissist, managing shared friendships, anticipating smear campaigns, and cultivating fresh, healthy social connections becomes paramount. The reflective exercises provided aim to be your guiding light, encouraging introspection and strategic foresight.

Yet, as we move forward, let's not forget that the path ahead, while promising, isn't without its thorns. Challenges will arise, but they are but stepping stones leading to your rebirth. The upcoming chapter offers a deeper exploration into rebuilding yourself post-separation, focusing on rediscovering your identity, strengths, and passions. Like the Phoenix, you too will find renewal, soaring to new heights with wings unfurled and spirit undaunted. Until then, remember, your resilience is your compass, and brighter days lie ahead.

8

THE FLIGHT

REBUILDING LIFE POST ABUSE

I remember standing on the precipice of a new dawn in my life. The weight of my relationship with the malignant narcissist still pressed on my shoulders, like the remnants of a long winter's night. One day, while on a solitary walk through the woods, I chanced upon a clearing. The rays of the morning sun warmed my skin, and the vibrant colors of blooming wildflowers painted the ground. I realized I too had an opportunity to rise from the ashes of my past. The path to that sunrise involved a tapestry of healing methods, each adding its own hue to the dawn of my new life.

Therapy: The first step for many on the road to recovery is seeking professional help. Therapists and counselors, trained in understanding the intricacies of narcissistic abuse, can offer invaluable guidance. They provide a safe space to process traumas, understand patterns, and develop coping mechanisms. Moreover, cognitive-behavioral therapy (CBT) can assist in reframing negative thought patterns, and trauma-focused therapy can address deep-seated wounds from the abuse.

Self-care routines: Healing is as much about the body as it is about the mind. Regular exercise, a balanced diet, and adequate rest are cornerstones of physical well-being. For me, yoga became a bridge connecting my body and soul, helping me release stored tensions and cultivating a sense of peace.

Mindfulness and meditation: These practices anchor us in the present moment. Mindfulness teaches us to observe our thoughts and emotions without judgment, enabling us to detach from the chaotic memories of the past. Meditation, on the other hand, offers a sanctuary of stillness. With regular practice, it can be a potent tool in managing anxiety, fostering gratitude, and embracing the present.

The healing journey from narcissistic abuse is neither linear nor singular. It requires a blend of approaches, each addressing a unique facet of our being. By integrating therapy, self-care, and mindfulness practices, we not only heal the scars of the past but also fortify ourselves for the vibrant future awaiting us. As the Phoenix rises renewed from the ashes, so too can we soar high, basking in the warmth of our newfound strength and freedom.

Following my escape from the grasp of a malignant narcissist, I felt akin to a bird whose wings had been clipped—unable to recognize my reflection or trust in my own worth. Through time, I came to realize that the first step toward recovery was to reestablish that connection with myself, to relearn the art of self-love.

Understanding Self-Love and Self-Worth: Self-love isn't merely about pampering oneself with luxuries or indulgences; it's an intrinsic belief in one's worthiness and value. It's the understanding that you deserve happiness, respect, and peace just as much as anyone else. Conversely, self-worth is the recognition of one's intrinsic value. It's understanding that your worth isn't determined by external factors or others' perceptions but by your very existence.

Strategies to Cultivate Self-Love and Improved Self-Esteem:

1. Affirmations: Begin each day by looking in the mirror and speaking kindness to yourself. Affirmations like "I am worthy of love," "I am resilient," and "I am growing" can gradually reshape negative self-perceptions.
2. Engage in Activities that Celebrate You: Pursue hobbies and activities that make you feel alive and connected to yourself. Whether it's reading, painting, hiking, or dancing, these

activities are reminders of your passions and
capabilities.

3. Maintain a Gratitude Journal: By regularly
   listing things you appreciate about yourself
   and your life, you'll nurture a positive mindset
   and focus on strengths and achievements
   rather than perceived flaws or past traumas.

4. Seek Supportive Communities: Surround
   yourself with individuals who uplift and
   validate you. This can be support groups,
   therapy, or friends and family who recognize
   your worth and encourage your journey to
   self-love.

Prioritize Your Needs: In the shadow of a narcissist, it's easy to forget your own needs. Prioritizing yourself isn't selfish; it's essential. Listen to your body, mind,
and soul. Rest when you're tired, seek joy when you're
down, and nourish yourself with positive experiences.

Setting Personal Boundaries: Boundaries are a
manifestation of self-respect. Clearly define what is
acceptable and unacceptable behavior from others.
Remember, it's okay to say "no" and to distance yourself
from individuals or situations that threaten your peace.

Loving oneself unconditionally is an ongoing journey.
It requires patience, understanding, and, at times,
forgiveness. Amidst the backdrop of a narcissistic rela-

109

tionship, it's easy to misplace our self-worth. However, like the Phoenix, with time and care, we can emerge radiant, embracing the light of self-love and soaring towards a horizon filled with endless potential.

As the horizon beckoned and I ventured into the world of new relationships post-narcissistic abuse, I felt like a fledgling bird testing its wings. The thrill of newfound freedom mixed with trepidation, reminiscent of early flights unsure of the winds. The lessons learned from the past became the guiding stars, illuminating the path towards healthier, more respectful relationships.

Recognizing Warning Signs:

Being previously entwined with a narcissist makes one more attuned to the subtleties of manipulation and control. Here are some warning signs to be vigilant about:

1. Love Bombing: Overwhelming affection and attention at the start of a relationship, only to use it as leverage later.
2. Gaslighting: Manipulating someone into doubting their own reality or sanity.
3. Lack of Empathy: An inability to understand or share the feelings of another.
4. Controlling Behavior: This can manifest as dictating who you spend time with, checking your phone, or making decisions on your behalf without consultation.

5. Chronic Dishonesty: Consistent lying, even about inconsequential things, indicates a deeper problem.

Strategies for Healthy Relationships:

1. Trust Your Intuition: If something feels off, trust that feeling. Your intuition is the culmination of lived experiences and inherent wisdom.

2. Maintain Strong Boundaries: Clearly communicate your boundaries. A partner who respects and honors them is indicative of a healthy relationship.

3. Open Communication: Foster an environment where both partners can speak openly about their feelings, concerns, and aspirations.

4. Take It Slow: It's okay to take your time to get to know someone. Building trust is a process, not a one-time event.

5. Seek Feedback: Engage with trusted friends or family members about your new relationship. Sometimes, an external perspective can offer valuable insights.

6. Therapy and Counseling: Consider seeking therapy or counseling, both individually and as a couple. This provides tools and strategies to navigate challenges and ensure the

relationship remains respectful and
supportive.

Remember, everyone deserves a relationship that's
founded on mutual respect, understanding, and love.
By being vigilant, trusting your intuition, and staying
true to yourself, you can ensure your journey into new
relationships is healthy and fulfilling. Like the
Phoenix, having risen from the ashes of the past, you
now possess the strength, wisdom, and grace to soar
towards brighter horizons.

As you soar towards your new horizons, it's imperative
to take moments of introspection. Here are some questions and prompts to help you delve deep into your
thoughts, fostering clarity and understanding.

Holistic Healing Approaches:

- Which holistic healing approach resonates
  with you the most, and why?
- How have therapy or mindfulness practices
  helped you in your healing journey?
- What self-care routines have you established,
  and how do they impact your daily life?

Self-Love and Self-Worth:

- Describe a moment when you felt a deep sense of self-love. What triggered it, and how did it feel?
- How have your views on self-worth evolved since your experience with narcissistic abuse?
- List down five qualities that you love about yourself. How can you celebrate these qualities more in your daily life?

Navigating New Relationships:

- Reflect on a recent interaction or relationship. Were there any signs, either positive or negative, that stood out to you?
- What boundaries have you established in your new relationships? How have they been received and respected by others?
- Imagine a healthy, fulfilling relationship. What does it look like, and how does it make you feel?

General Reflections:

- Like the Phoenix, in what ways have you risen from the challenges of your past to become stronger and more resilient?
- What have been the most significant milestones in your healing journey so far?

- Visualize yourself a year from now. What progress do you hope to see, and what steps will you take to achieve that vision?

As you pen down your thoughts, imagine each word acting as a feather, adding strength to your wings. With every reflection, you're preparing for higher flights, charting courses through skies unknown. Embrace this process of introspection—it's your compass, guiding you towards healing, understanding, and growth.

In our journey through this chapter, we've journeyed along the trails of healing and rebirth. Much like a Phoenix, who emerges from the ashes brighter and more resplendent, every survivor of narcissistic abuse has the innate potential to soar to unprecedented heights.

Let's take a moment to reflect on what we've learned:

1. Holistic Healing Approaches: Therapy, self-care, mindfulness, and meditation are not just therapeutic modalities but lifelines that ground us, offering solace and structure as we navigate the tumultuous waves of recovery.

2. Self-Love and Self-Worth: Our value isn't defined by our past or by the words of another. By embracing self-love, setting boundaries, and recognizing our inherent worth, we set the stage for genuine healing and transformation.

3. Navigating New Relationships: The scars from our past experiences don't have to dictate our future connections. Armed with knowledge, self-awareness, and resilience, we can forge relationships founded on mutual respect, trust, and love.

Dear reader, as you close this chapter and perhaps even take a pause, know this: The journey of recovery is a marathon, not a sprint. Every step you take, no matter how small, is a testament to your resilience, strength, and indomitable spirit. I've walked this path, and I can assure you, every challenge faced, every tear shed, adds depth to your story and strength to your wings.

In our next chapter, we'll delve deeper into the transformational power of resilience. We'll explore the concept of post-traumatic growth and how adversities, as harsh as they may seem, can shape us, refine us, and lead us to discover strengths we never knew we possessed. Keep soaring, for the sky is not your limit but your starting point.

THE PHOENIX'S PLUMAGE

REDISCOVERING AND NURTURING YOUR PERSONAL INTERESTS POST ABUSE

The sun was setting, casting a warm, golden hue over the beach. I found myself standing there, barefoot, with a sketchbook in hand. It had been years since I had drawn anything, even though sketching by the sea used to be my favorite pastime. As I began to move my pencil, memories flooded back of a time before I met my narcissistic partner—a time when my interests, however small or large, were a genuine reflection of my identity. Drawing at the beach was more than just a hobby; it was a part of me. But over the years, under his shadow, that part was stifled and nearly forgotten. As the waves crashed against the shore, I felt a profound realization: while I may have set aside my sketchbook, my passions, much like the Phoenix, were ready to be reborn from the ashes.

In the world of a narcissist, the central figure is always themselves. Their needs, desires, and interests take center stage, while others, particularly their partners, become mere supporting roles—sometimes even pushed off the stage entirely.

One of the most disheartening tactics used by narcissists is to belittle or outright suppress their partner's passions and hobbies. But why? Why would someone want to stifle the very aspects of a person that make them unique and vibrant?

From a psychological perspective, narcissists often operate from a place of profound insecurity, even if they outwardly display overwhelming confidence. When their partner exhibits independence or individuality—whether that's through pursuing personal hobbies or simply enjoying time alone—it becomes a potential threat to the narcissist's fragile self-worth. If you're thriving without them or have an aspect of life where they are not the focal point, it introduces the terrifying notion (for the narcissist) that they might not be indispensable.

Furthermore, narcissists thrive on control. By diminishing your interests, they seek to create an environment where you're more dependent on them, both emotionally and mentally. This control tactic ensures that they remain the dominant figure in the relationship, with you perpetually seeking their validation.

Another reason lies in the narcissist's need for constant attention and admiration. Personal pursuits often divert attention away from them, leading to feelings of jealousy and resentment. In their skewed perspective, every moment you spend on your hobby is a moment not spent admiring or attending to them.

In essence, the suppression of a partner's passions by a narcissist is a complex interplay of their insecurities, need for control, and insatiable desire for attention. Understanding this can be the first step in reclaiming the parts of yourself that were overshadowed. Like the Phoenix, your passions, once suppressed, can rise again —burning even brighter than before.

As we delve into the understanding of the narcissist's suppressive tendencies, it's essential to remember that beneath their overpowering shadow, the radiant plumage of your individuality still exists. It may have been dulled or overshadowed for a while, but each feather—each passion and interest—awaits rediscovery. Let's embark on a gentle journey to uncover these lost treasures of your soul.

A Journey Within: Rediscovering Your Passions

1. Find a Quiet Space: Begin by finding a serene place where you can sit undisturbed, perhaps surrounded by nature, or in a cozy corner of your home. Breathe deeply, allowing yourself to be present in the moment.
2. Visualize Your Younger Self: Close your eyes and picture yourself in a time before the

narcissistic relationship. What were you doing? Where were you? Recall the clothes you wore, the activities you engaged in, and the dreams you held.

3. List Down Memories: With your eyes still closed, let your mind wander through the gallery of your memories. Every time an activity or interest sparks a sense of joy or nostalgia, make a mental note of it.

4. Journaling: Open your eyes and jot down the memories and activities that came to mind. Don't censor or judge anything—whether it was painting, hiking, reading, or even just daydreaming under a tree.

5. Dreams Unfulfilled: Apart from recalling old hobbies, also ponder upon the dreams and interests you never pursued due to fear, lack of time, or the narcissist's influence. Maybe you wanted to learn a musical instrument or take up dancing.

6. Feeling the Emotions: As you list these activities, take a moment to acknowledge how each one makes you feel. Is there excitement? Longing? Maybe even a tinge of sadness for the time lost? These emotions are signposts, guiding you towards what your soul truly craves.

7. Creating a Vision Board: If you're a visual person, consider creating a vision board. Attach pictures, quotes, or anything else that

resonates with your rediscovered interests.
Place this board somewhere you can see daily,
serving as a constant reminder and
motivation.

Engaging in this reflective exercise can be profoundly moving. It's a rendezvous with the self that was momentarily lost but is eager to shine again. As you look at your list or vision board, remember that these passions, like the Phoenix's feathers, are integral to your radiant identity. They hold the power to not only heal but to elevate you to newer heights of self-awareness and joy.

As a psychologist, I've seen time and again the transformative power that personal interests and hobbies have on an individual's mental and emotional well-being. Like the Phoenix, which undergoes renewal by fire, delving into these personal pursuits can lead to rejuvenation and rebirth. Let's explore the therapeutic foundations of this phenomenon.

Rebuilding Self-Esteem

- Evidence-based Benefits: Research in clinical psychology indicates that engaging in hobbies boosts one's self-concept. When we immerse ourselves in an activity we love, it offers a sense of mastery. Every painting completed, every song learned, every book read adds a layer of accomplishment and affirms our capabilities.

- Safe Exploration: Hobbies provide a safe space for trial and error. Unlike other domains in life where mistakes might have bigger consequences, personal interests allow for exploration without significant risks. Every mistake becomes a learning opportunity, and every success, no matter how small, becomes a pillar for self-confidence.

Fostering Positive Emotions

- Flow and Mindfulness: Dr. Mihaly Csikszentmihalyi's research on the concept of 'flow'—that deeply engaged state where we lose track of time and are wholly absorbed in the task—emphasizes how hobbies can be a direct gateway to this enriching experience. Being in the flow combats feelings of anxiety and boosts happiness.
- Positive Reinforcement: Engaging in hobbies leads to the release of dopamine, the 'feel good' neurotransmitter. Over time, the brain starts associating these activities with positive emotions, creating a virtuous cycle. The more we engage, the better we feel.

Creating a Sense of Accomplishment

- Tangible Results: Hobbies, especially those that have a tangible end product—like painting, crafting, or gardening—offer visible proof of our efforts. These creations are not just artifacts but symbols of dedication, patience, and skill.
- Setting and Achieving Goals: The structure of most hobbies involves setting small goals. Achieving these, be it finishing a knitting project or mastering a difficult yoga pose, gives a profound sense of accomplishment. According to positive psychology findings, setting and achieving such micro-goals consistently boosts one's overall sense of purpose and direction in life.
- Social Validation: Sharing our achievements, whether with a close-knit circle or a larger community, often brings in validation. While the pursuit of hobbies isn't primarily for external validation, the appreciation received can further solidify feelings of self-worth.

In essence, our personal interests are not just pastimes —they're lifelines to our deepest selves. They anchor us in moments of turmoil and lift us in times of joy. As you soar through your healing journey, embracing these interests is akin to the Phoenix flapping its powerful wings, rising higher with each beat. Remember, every stroke of the brush, every note played, every step taken in dance is a testament to your resilience and the beauty you're capable of creating.

It's a heartwarming experience to think of the Phoenix reacquainting with the elements that once fueled its flight. In much the same way, rekindling our connection with past hobbies can serve as a beacon of light, illuminating our journey forward. The question is, how do we reengage with these once-beloved activities, especially after a hiatus induced by circumstances out of our control? Here are some practical steps to guide your return:

1. Start Small and Set Realistic Goals:

- How: Begin with shorter sessions of your hobby, be it 15 minutes of sketching, reading a few pages of a novel, or playing an instrument. Over time, gradually increase the duration.
- Benefits: This approach reduces feelings of overwhelm and sets the stage for consistent, sustainable progress. Every completed session reinforces your self-efficacy and commitment.

2. Dedicate "Me Time":

- How: Set aside specific times in the week dedicated solely to your hobby. Mark it in your calendar, and treat it with as much importance as any other appointment.

- Benefits: This structure ensures regular engagement, and over time, this scheduled "me time" becomes a cherished sanctuary, a space of solace and joy amidst the hustle of daily life.

3. Join a Club or Group:

- How: Local community centers, libraries, or even cafes often host clubs or workshops related to various hobbies. Seek them out and become a member.
- Benefits: Being part of a group fosters a sense of community, offers mutual encouragement, and presents opportunities to learn from others. This sense of belonging can greatly amplify the joy derived from the hobby.

4. Explore Online Communities:

- How: Platforms like Meetup, Reddit, or specialized forums cater to virtually every hobby imaginable. These digital spaces can be treasure troves of resources, advice, and camaraderie.
- Benefits: Engaging with like-minded enthusiasts from around the world can

provide a broader perspective, invaluable tips, and the heartwarming realization that you're not alone in your passion.

5. Celebrate Milestones:

- How: Every time you reach a personal goal related to your hobby, take a moment to acknowledge it. It could be as simple as writing in a journal or sharing it with a friend.
- Benefits: Recognizing your achievements, however small, nurtures a positive feedback loop, motivating you to engage more and push your boundaries.

6. Stay Open to Evolution:

- How: As you reengage, allow your approach to the hobby to evolve. Maybe you painted landscapes before, but now you're drawn to abstracts. Embrace the change.
- Benefits: This fluidity ensures that the hobby remains a source of joy and not a rigid chore. It's a reflection of your growth and the new chapters in your life story.

In essence, as you reconnect with your past interests, you're not just engaging in a hobby; you're embracing fragments of your essence that were temporarily lost.

Like the Phoenix, drawing strength from its vibrant plumage, you too will rediscover the hues that make you uniquely you, celebrating every shade and texture. And in this journey of reconnection, you fortify your identity, ensuring that it shines brilliantly against any backdrop.

Each phase of the Phoenix's journey brings forth a renewed vitality, an invigorated spirit that soars to greater heights. Similarly, our foray into unexplored terrains of hobbies and interests can lead to unparalleled growth and joy. Exploring unfamiliar passions is akin to opening doors to rooms within ourselves we never knew existed. The thrill of novelty, combined with the innate human drive to learn, can be deeply fulfilling.

As you stand at this crossroads of rediscovery, I urge you to embrace the audacity of new beginnings. Venture beyond the boundaries of familiarity, and let the siren song of curiosity lead the way. Here's a curated list of potential hobbies, each bringing its unique shade of joy:

1. Creative Writing:

Benefits: Expressing your thoughts, emotions, and imaginations through words can be therapeutic. It fosters introspection, enhances vocabulary, and provides an avenue for cathartic release.

2. Photography:

Benefits: Through the lens, you learn to observe the world with greater detail, finding beauty in the mundane. It enhances mindfulness and cultivates an appreciation for the world around you.

3. Dance:

Benefits: Beyond the obvious physical advantages, dancing is a celebration of the human spirit. It improves coordination, boosts mood, and connects you to various cultures and rhythms.

4. Gardening:

Benefits: Tending to plants grounds you—literally and metaphorically. It teaches patience, offers sensory delights, and fosters a connection with the Earth.

5. Pottery or Sculpting:

Benefits: Shaping clay or other materials engages the tactile senses and offers a tangible output of your creative process. It enhances dexterity and offers meditative moments of focus.

6. Outdoor Sports (like hiking or kayaking):

Benefits: Such activities provide cardiovascular benefits, boost endorphins, and connect you with nature, offering moments of reflection amidst the vastness of the natural world.

7. Learning a Musical Instrument:

Benefits: Beyond the joy of creating melodies, learning an instrument enhances cognitive functions, improves memory, and fosters discipline.

8. Cooking or Baking:

Benefits: These are sensory-rich hobbies that culminate in delightful tastes. They offer creative outlets and the joy of sharing your culinary creations with loved ones.

9. Astronomy:

Benefits: Gazing at stars and planets fosters a sense of wonder and humility. It provides perspective and connects you to the vastness of the cosmos.

10. Crafts (like knitting, jewelry making, or DIY projects):

Benefits: Crafts enhance hand-eye coordination, fuel creativity, and provide tangible results that can be sources of pride.

As you embark on these new adventures, remember that the essence lies in the journey, not just the destination. It's about the exhilaration of the first step, the wonder of the first note, the pride in the first creation. Embracing new hobbies is an affirmation of life's boundless possibilities. In each endeavor, you weave a new thread into the rich tapestry of your life, adding layers of experiences, knowledge, and joy. Like the Phoenix, constantly reborn from its ashes, let each new interest be a testament to your indomitable spirit's ability to rise, learn, and celebrate life's myriad hues.

As the Phoenix takes its maiden flight after its rebirth, each beat of its wings, each glint of the sun on its newly-formed plumage is a cause for celebration. This journey of exploration and self-discovery is dotted with myriad milestones, each deserving of acknowledgment and pride. Reveling in the small joys and accomplishments serves as a reminder of your resilience, growth, and progress.

However, the path of rediscovery, like that of the Phoenix, isn't without its challenges. The initial excitement of embarking on a new hobby or revisiting an old one can, at times, be eclipsed by feelings of inadequacy or frustration. Maybe the paintbrush doesn't move as smoothly as you remembered, or the chords of a musical instrument sound discordant after years of disuse. Understandably, when faced with such obstacles, feelings of self-doubt can creep in.

It's essential to remember, though, that these moments are not indicative of your worth or capabilities. They're merely part of the learning curve—a testament to your courage in embracing the unknown or the long-forgotten. Here are some strategies to keep the flame of motivation burning brightly:

Set Micro-goals: Instead of aiming for perfection from the get-go, set small, achievable targets. Celebrating these mini-achievements can propel you forward and boost your confidence.

Practice Mindfulness: When faced with frustration, take a moment to breathe deeply, center yourself, and re-engage with the task with a calm mind. Often, our own expectations and pressures are the root of our anxieties.

Embrace the Learner's Mindset: Remember, every expert was once a beginner. Adopt a curious, open mindset where mistakes are seen as opportunities for growth, not as failures.

Seek a Supportive Community: Whether it's joining a club, attending workshops, or participating in online forums, surrounding yourself with like-minded individuals can provide encouragement, guidance, and a sense of camaraderie.

Document Your Journey: Keeping a journal of your progress, complete with photos or notes, can serve as a tangible reminder of how far you've come. On days when you feel stuck, revisiting these entries can reignite your passion.

Be Kind to Yourself: Celebrate the fact that you're trying, that you're pushing boundaries, and that you're committed to personal growth. A dose of self-compassion can go a long way in assuaging feelings of inadequacy.

The Phoenix, in its resplendent glory, is revered not just for its beauty but for its journey of rebirth and resilience. In much the same way, your journey is not defined by the challenges you face but by how you rise above them, adding depth and richness to your life's tapestry. Every brushstroke, every note, every step you take is a declaration of your spirit's strength and tenacity. Celebrate it, cherish it, and keep soaring.

As the Phoenix displays its radiant plumage, its magnificence serves as a symbol of hope and rebirth. In a similar vein, when we find passions that enliven our spirit, revealing them to the world can be a transformative experience both for ourselves and those around us.

Sharing isn't merely an act of exhibiting our interests; it has a profound impact on the fabric of human connection. When we allow our story to be witnessed, we receive affirmation and validation. The feedback and encouragement from others fortify our confidence and underscore the significance of our pursuits. This act of opening up paves the way for forging stronger bonds. Our passions become a bridge, connecting us deeper with friends, family, and sometimes even acquaintances. These shared interests can lead to collaborative endeavors, solidify lifelong friendships, or reinvigorate relationships that had waned over time.

But beyond personal connections, our stories of rediscovery and passion have a broader influence. They become sources of inspiration. Just by embodying the tale of a person who rose, found solace, and joy amidst challenges, we become the beacon someone else might need to embark on their path of self-discovery. Our resilience, shared openly, becomes an empowerment tool for others, nudging them to seek their passions and break free from whatever holds them back.

Furthermore, in this journey of sharing, we often find that we're not isolated in our experiences. We connect with communities of like-minded souls, providing both solace and exhilaration in shared joys and challenges. Within these communities, there's an organic shift from mere participation to a more active role. Many find healing in guiding others, as teaching becomes a profound source of fulfillment, a way to revisit and reinforce personal learnings.

And finally, every story we share, every passion we unveil, leaves an indelible mark. It becomes part of a narrative that future generations might draw inspiration from. Our journeys, our struggles, and our joys become beacons, signaling hope and the promise of rebirth.

In today's interconnected world, there are myriad ways to share — from personal interactions, workshops, to digital platforms. Whether it's a single photo, a recounting of a challenge surmounted, or a deep dive into our experiences, every shared fragment has the potential to resonate deeply with someone else.

In embracing and displaying our passions, we don't just validate our experiences; we illuminate the paths for countless others, reminding them, and ourselves, that rejuvenation, rebirth, and rediscovery are within reach for all.

The mythical Phoenix, in all its splendor, is not simply a creature of radiant beauty. Each hue, each feather in its magnificent plumage, tells a story of endurance, transformation, and rebirth. Just as the Phoenix rises from its ashes, more brilliant and fiery than before, so too have you embarked on a journey of self-reclamation, rising from the remnants of past struggles.

Your passions, interests, and pursuits are akin to the individual feathers of the Phoenix. They are markers of your resilience, symbols of your inherent vibrancy, and they encapsulate the essence of your soul. Each time you dive deep into an old hobby or venture into a new interest, you're adding a new hue to your life's tapestry, making it richer, more varied, and unequivocally yours.

In the wake of challenges, especially after surviving narcissistic abuse, rediscovering and embracing these passions has allowed you to not just heal but to flourish. It's given you a palette to paint your narrative anew, to define your identity on your terms, and to reclaim the joy that rightfully belongs to you.

As the Phoenix soars the skies, its fiery trail is a testament to its incredible journey. Let your passions and interests be the trail you leave behind, reminding both you and the world of your strength, your uniqueness, and your capability to transform adversities into unparalleled beauty.

Wear your plumage with pride, dear reader. Celebrate the colors that make you who you are. And as you continue to explore the vast skies of possibilities, remember to bask in every moment, every discovery, for you are, in every sense, a Phoenix reborn, soaring towards endless horizons.

10

SOARING HIGH

HEALING AND MOVING FORWARD

The sun was dipping below the horizon, casting a warm golden hue over the park. As I sat on a bench, book in hand, a gentle breeze rustled the pages, beckoning my attention away from the text. Gazing at the children playing nearby and families sharing laughter, a poignant memory surfaced.

Years ago, in the aftermath of escaping my narcissistic relationship, I found myself in a similar park setting. But back then, everything felt like a blurred, surreal painting. My surroundings appeared familiar, yet internally, I felt like a stranger in my own life. The world was moving, but I felt stagnant, unsure of who I was or what I truly wanted.

Coming back to the present, with the clarity of healing and introspection, I recognized the journey I had undertaken - the journey from ashes to my own phoenix self. It's a journey I've seen countless of my clients take, finding their way back to their true selves after the shattering experience of narcissistic abuse. This chapter is dedicated to that courageous voyage.

Emerging from a narcissistic relationship can feel like waking up from a long, disorienting dream. The relationship, with its complex manipulation tactics, often leaves victims disengaged from their own identity. However, rediscovering who you are beneath the layers of pain and confusion is a cornerstone of healing and rebuilding.

1. Embrace Solitude: Before diving back into the social world, grant yourself the gift of solitude. Spend time alone, absorbing the silence and being present with your thoughts. Solitude can be a sanctuary where you reacquaint yourself with your passions, dreams, and desires.

2. Reflect on Your Values: Take a moment to list down your core values. What truly matters to you? What principles do you want to uphold? Narcissistic relationships often involve compromising our values to keep the peace. Realigning with them helps rebuild a sense of self.

3. Engage in Self-Expression: Whether it's through art, journaling, music, or dance, expressing yourself can be incredibly therapeutic. It's not about producing a

masterpiece but about letting your innermost feelings find a voice.

4. Set Small, Achievable Goals: Begin with simple tasks or activities that you once enjoyed. Whether it's reading a book, taking a short walk, or trying out a new recipe, these small victories can bolster your confidence.

5. Seek External Perspectives: Sometimes, talking to trusted friends or family can offer valuable insights. They can remind you of strengths you've forgotten or qualities you've overlooked.

Remember, the phoenix rises from the ashes, reborn, resilient, and radiant. As you work through the aftermath of narcissistic abuse, envision yourself as this magnificent bird, ever-evolving and soaring to new heights. Your identity, once obscured, will shine brightly once more.

In nature, even the mighty oak tree relies on the nurturing elements surrounding it to grow tall and strong. Similarly, after the storm of narcissistic abuse, the nurturing environment provided by a steadfast support system is paramount for recovery. It acts as the sunshine that warms us, the rain that hydrates our roots, and the soil that offers strength and foundation.

One might wonder, why is a support system so crucial? The answer lies in the very nature of narcissistic abuse. Such relationships often leave one feeling isolated, doubting their reality and even their sanity. This is where a supportive circle steps in, validating experiences, offering encouragement, and reminding the survivor of their inherent worth.

To cultivate such a circle, it's essential first to recognize what a healthy relationship looks like. True supportive relationships are mutual, where respect, understanding, and compassion flow both ways. They do not echo the patterns of dominance, manipulation, or conditional affection often seen in narcissistic relationships.

Seeking professional help is a formidable step in the recovery journey. Therapists, especially those specialized in trauma or personality disorders, bring a combination of academic knowledge and clinical insight. They offer structured guidance and tools that empower one to process their experience and chart a way forward. For me, my therapeutic journey was akin to having a beacon of light, guiding me through the darkest tunnels of my past.

Support groups, whether in-person or online, offer a unique sense of solidarity. Engaging with others who've faced similar experiences can be immensely validating. It reminds survivors they aren't alone and offers a platform for shared healing. There's an unparalleled strength in collective resilience, in stories of triumph that inspire and uplift.

Lastly, reaching out to friends and family might seem daunting, especially if the narcissistic relationship had strained those ties. Yet, genuine relationships can withstand storms and rebuild. Open conversations, transparency about one's journey, and shared moments of understanding can revive these vital connections.

In essence, building a robust support system is about intertwining with others in a dance of mutual growth and care. Like a Phoenix that draws strength from its community, your circle will lift you, supporting your flight towards healing and rediscovery.

After the final fiery clash with a narcissistic partner, the cooling embers might beckon you back, either out of habit, lingering emotions, or the narcissist's manipulations. However, just like the Phoenix, rebirth demands a departure from the old, a kind of detachment that allows new growth. In the context of narcissistic abuse, this often translates to establishing No Contact or, when unavoidable, Low Contact strategies.

No Contact: This strategy is akin to a forest after a fire, allowing nature to restore itself without any external interference. It's about creating an environment free from the narcissist's influence, permitting genuine healing to take root.

1. Digital Detox: One of the first steps involves severing digital connections. Block them from social media, delete their number, and filter their emails. This not only prevents them from reaching out but also stops you from

seeking updates about their life, which can hinder emotional detachment.

2. Change Your Routines: Narcissists are adept at tracking patterns. If you've frequented certain places or followed specific schedules, consider altering them, even if momentarily. This reduces the chances of accidental run-ins.

3. Inform Close Contacts: Let friends and family know about your decision to maintain no contact. Their understanding and support can act as additional layers of defense against potential manipulations by the narcissist.

Low Contact: In some situations, going completely no contact might be infeasible, especially if there are shared responsibilities like children or business engagements. Here, the strategy is to minimize interaction, keeping it succinct and devoid of personal emotions, similar to a Phoenix that flies high, engaging with the ground only when necessary.

1. Set Clear Boundaries: Determine the specific reasons for needed contact and stick to them. If it's about children, keep conversations strictly related to their well-being. If it's work, discuss only professional matters.

2. Choose Neutral Meeting Places: If in-person meetings are unavoidable, select public or neutral locations. This not only provides a

sense of security but can also deter potential outbursts or manipulative tactics.

3. Document Interactions: Keeping a record of communications can serve as evidence if the narcissist tries to manipulate or gaslight. It's also a means of self-assurance, a tangible reminder of your experiences.

The journey of maintaining distance from a narcissistic ex-partner isn't without its challenges. There might be moments of doubt, where the memories of good times overshadow the pain. There could be external pressures, perhaps from mutual acquaintances or societal expectations. And then there's the narcissist's own toolkit of manipulations, from guilt trips to charm offensives or even threats.

Facing these challenges requires a blend of inner fortitude and external support. Recognize the moments of weakness, lean on your support circle, and, if needed, seek therapeutic guidance. Always remember, like the Phoenix, the intensity of the flames you've endured has only fortified you, granting you the strength and wisdom to guard your space and thrive.

Journaling is a powerful tool, much like a gentle river stream that gradually shapes the mighty stones within its path. As you reflect and write, the process can help you unearth deeply buried emotions, offer clarity, and set a course for the future. The Phoenix, too, in its moments of solitude, contemplates the depths of its fiery existence, preparing for the next ascent. Here are some reflective questions and prompts to guide you:

1. Past Reflections

- Describe a moment in your past relationship where you felt most distant from your true self. How did it feel?
- Recall a moment when you felt a spark of your identity, even amidst the turmoil. What caused that spark?

2. Evaluating Progress

- Since distancing yourself from the narcissistic relationship, list three emotions or experiences you've felt more deeply or frequently. Are these emotions indicating growth or areas needing attention?
- Describe a recent situation where you successfully set a boundary. How did it differ from past encounters?

3. Reassessing Goals

- Envision your life a year from now. What do you see? What steps can lead you to that vision?
- Think about the personal attributes you'd like to strengthen post-recovery. How can your

newfound knowledge and experiences aid in this development?

4. Strategizing Future Actions

- What potential triggers or challenges do you foresee in maintaining No Contact or Low Contact? How can you prepare for them?
- List down people, resources, or activities that consistently make you feel empowered and grounded. How can you integrate them more into your life?

5. The Phoenix Perspective

- Imagine you are the Phoenix, observing your life from a soaring height. What patterns or insights become evident from this vantage point?
- The Phoenix is reborn from its ashes. If you were to pick one symbol or metaphor for your rebirth, what would it be and why?

Journaling doesn't demand perfection. It asks for authenticity. Your journal is a sacred space, a dialogue between your past self, the present you, and the future self you're nurturing. Let the words flow, let emotions unravel, and as the pages fill, may you find the clarity and strength to chart your path forward. Remember, every reflection is a step closer to your Phoenix moment of rebirth and soaring.

The journey you've embarked on, dear reader, is not just about moving away from the ashes of an oppressive past but also about soaring towards a future full of promise and self-realization. The Phoenix, in its splendor, represents not just rebirth but also the brilliance of a life lived authentically. In this chapter, we delved deep into the process of rebuilding your life after experiencing a narcissistic relationship. The essence of rediscovery is not just about returning to who you once were but embracing the evolved, stronger version of yourself.

The scaffolding of a renewed life heavily rests upon the supportive pillars of family, friends, and sometimes professionals who lend their strength and wisdom. Their role isn't to define your journey but to walk beside you, reminding you of your inherent worth. And while there might be days where the temptation to revert to old habits or connections feels strong, remember the strategies discussed for maintaining No Contact or Low Contact. They are essential, not just as protective barriers but as affirmations of your commitment to your well-being.

The reflections and journaling exercises serve as your compass, helping navigate the vast landscape of emotions and aspirations. They offer an intimate space for dialogues, dreams, and determination, fostering clarity in the maze of recovery.

As we transition to the subsequent chapters, we'll delve deeper into the intricacies of self-love, the nuances of emotional well-being, and the art of thriving, not just surviving. Just like the Phoenix, you are destined to rise, to shine, and to illuminate. Embrace the journey, for every beat of your wings echoes the resilience of your spirit and the promise of brighter horizons. Onward, dear reader, to new beginnings and boundless skies.

11

THE NEW HORIZON

AVOIDING NARCISSISTS AND FOSTERING HEALTHY RELATIONSHIPS

The warm rays of a setting sun bathed the horizon in hues of gold and amber. I found myself on a solitary walk along the beach, my thoughts heavy with the memories of my relationship with a malignant narcissist. As the waves kissed the shore, an elderly woman approached me, her silver hair dancing in the wind. We exchanged pleasantries, and as our conversation deepened, she shared her own story of escaping a toxic relationship many years ago. Her eyes sparkled with wisdom, "Young lady," she began, "like the tides, life has its ebbs and flows. But always remember, if you can recognize the storm on the horizon, you can steer clear before it engulfs you."

Our conversation stayed with me, reminding me of the immense importance of recognizing the signs of potential harm. Like the gathering clouds that warn of an impending storm, there are discernible signs and behavior patterns in people that might point towards narcissistic tendencies.

In my two decades of clinical practice, I've encountered numerous stories that echo familiar patterns. For instance, consider Jamie, a client of mine, who entered into a new relationship filled with whirlwind romance. The intensity and charm were overwhelming at first, often referred to as "love bombing" in psychological circles. But, as the weeks turned into months, she began to notice a pattern where her partner would belittle her achievements and make her feel small. Research has shown that narcissists often use tactics like gaslighting—a form of persistent manipulation and brainwashing that causes the victim to doubt themselves—to maintain control.

Another sign that is supported by numerous studies is a chronic lack of empathy. Sarah, another individual I worked with, often recounted how her partner seemed incapable of understanding or sharing her feelings. This emotional void, she realized, was not the norm but rather a glaring red flag pointing to his narcissistic tendencies.

But amidst these signs, one of the most crucial lessons is to trust our own instincts. Our intuition, that gut feeling, is a powerful tool that has evolved over millennia. When something doesn't feel right, it probably isn't. It's essential to remember that recognizing these signs is not about judging or labeling someone but about ensuring our own emotional well-being.

Drawing boundaries becomes paramount here. Imagine your heart, your emotions, and your self-esteem as a cherished garden. Just as you wouldn't allow harmful pests to ruin it, it's essential to guard against those who might trample upon your emotional well-being. Boundaries act as that protective fence, ensuring that while you let in love, respect, and kindness, you keep out toxicity and harm.

The journey ahead is about fostering relationships that nurture your soul and steer clear of those that deplete it. Like the wise woman on the beach once told me, recognizing the storm is the first step in avoiding it. And remember, dear reader, like the Phoenix, you have risen from the ashes once, and you have the strength and wisdom to soar above any storm that might come your way.

Relationships, in their purest essence, are like intricately designed castles. Each brick is placed with care, intention, and mutual effort. Building these magnificent structures requires patience, understanding, and, most importantly, a blueprint of the fundamental principles that uphold their strength and beauty.

One of the cornerstone principles is open and transparent communication. Much like the foundation of a castle needs to be robust and unyielding, so does the communication in a relationship. Engaging in open dialogues where both parties feel heard and under-stood is essential. This involves actively listening without interrupting, validating each other's feelings, and practicing non-defensive responses. For instance, if a partner mentions feeling neglected, instead of imme-diately becoming defensive, one might say, "I'm sorry you feel that way. Can we discuss what's been making you feel neglected so I can understand better?"

Closely tied to communication is the art of setting and maintaining boundaries. Think of these as the protec-tive walls of your castle. Everyone has their comfort zones, limits, and personal spaces, both physically and emotionally. By vocalizing what's acceptable and what's not, you not only protect your well-being but also provide clarity to your partner. An example might be letting a partner know that you need some time alone after work to unwind and recharge. It's not a rejection of them but a way to ensure you're at your best when you're together.

Mutual respect is the grand archway leading into the castle. In the words of Albert Einstein, "Every human being, of whatever origin, of whatever station, deserves respect. We must each respect others even as we respect ourselves." This implies recognizing the inherent worth and feelings of the other person. If you envision a relationship as a dance, respect ensures both partners move harmoniously, celebrating each step, avoiding stepping on each other's toes, and guiding one another through the rhythm of life.

Understanding is the lush garden within the castle's boundaries. It's where empathy blooms and compassion flourishes. To truly understand is to place oneself in the shoes of the other, feeling their joys, their pains, their aspirations. It's about recognizing that every individual is a vast universe of experiences, memories, and dreams. So when conflicts arise, as they often do, seeking to understand before being understood can be a transformative approach.

Lastly, kindness is the gentle river flowing beside this castle, ever-constant, ever-nurturing. Small acts of kindness, whether it's a comforting word, a warm hug, or simply being there for someone, can reinforce the bond and bridge any divides.

In your journey, it's vital to remember that just as every brick in a castle matters, so does every gesture, word, and intention in a relationship. You, dear reader, are deserving of a relationship that mirrors the grandeur and warmth of the most magnificent castles — where respect, kindness, and mutual growth reign supreme. Like the Phoenix, you've known the ashes, but now, it's time for you to bask in the glow of relationships that elevate and celebrate you.

Your journey doesn't end with overcoming hardships. True growth occurs when you commit to continuous self-improvement and nurturing of your soul. Continuous self-improvement is the gentle art of acknowledging that while you've come a long way, there's always room to flourish further. You are not defined by your past, but shaped by your present actions and future aspirations.

Pursuing a hobby, for instance, not only fosters creativity but can be a powerful conduit for self-expression. Whether it's painting, writing, dancing, or any other form of art, it allows our soul to convey stories, emotions, and dreams in ways words sometimes cannot. Beyond artistic pursuits, hobbies like gardening can connect us to the Earth, reminding us of the cycles of life, growth, decay, and rebirth.

Seeking therapy is another avenue of profound self-growth. Just as we consult a physician for our physical ailments, our minds too, on occasion, need that professional touch. Therapists provide tools, insights, and perspectives that empower us to navigate life's complexities with resilience and clarity.

Support groups are havens of shared experiences. Being in a space where individuals understand your journey, having walked similar paths, can be immensely comforting. It's a reminder that you're not alone, and collective wisdom can often light the way when the path seems obscured.

Practicing mindfulness and meditation are not just buzzwords in today's fast-paced world; they're anchors that help ground us. These practices teach us to live in the present moment, to cherish it, and to find peace within, even when external storms rage.

While these are all instrumental activities, it's essential to understand that the core of self-care and self-improvement is a mindset. It's the unwavering belief in one's own worth, potential, and the understanding that our well-being is both a right and a responsibility.

To you, dear reader, always remember: your journey is an eternal one. You've risen from the ashes, and now the vast skies beckon. Spread your wings of self-care and personal growth, and soar towards the horizons of your dreams. Embrace every gust of wind, every ray of sun, and even the impending storms, for they all contribute to the majesty of your flight. The universe, in all its vastness, is both your playground and your sanctuary. Keep flying, for the world needs your light.

To help you on this endeavor, use these reflections and prompts, let the pen (or keyboard) be the vessel through which your soul speaks. Dive deep, for within its depths lie insights that pave the path to a brighter, more resilient future.

Reflections:

- The Phoenix's Flight: Imagine yourself as a bird, soaring above a vast landscape. What do you see below? How does the wind feel beneath your wings? By visualizing this, you connect with the strength and freedom inherent within you.

- Defining Growth: What does personal growth mean to you? Is it gaining new skills, fostering deeper relationships, or perhaps, understanding oneself better?
- Anchors of Stability: Reflect upon the activities or routines that ground you, especially during turbulent times. How can you incorporate more of these moments into your daily life?

Journal Prompts:

- The Joy of Hobbies: Write about a hobby you've always wanted to explore but never did. What draws you to it? Commit to taking a small step towards pursuing it this week.
- The Healing Power of Sharing: Think about a time when sharing your story, whether in a support group or with a trusted friend, brought you relief or clarity. If you haven't shared yet, write about the fears or reservations holding you back.
- Mindfulness Moments: Describe a moment from the past week where you were fully present. How did it feel? What sensations, emotions, or thoughts do you remember from it?
- Boundaries and Respect: Reflect on your current relationships. Are there any where you feel your boundaries are not respected?

How can you communicate or reinforce these boundaries better?

- The Next Horizon: Visualize where you want to be in a year. Describe this future in vivid detail – the environment, the people, your feelings, and even the challenges. What steps can you take in the present to move closer to this vision?

In the vast tapestry of our lives, every thread holds significance, weaving together to create the magnificent portrait of who we are. This chapter took you on a journey from recognizing the subtle yet profound signs of narcissistic behaviors to the sanctity of cultivating enriching relationships. It emphasized the sacred practice of self-improvement and continuous care.

You have equipped yourself with the knowledge and insights to not just identify potential harm but to also champion the nurturing of genuine, loving relationships. More than anything, I hope you've come to recognize the vast reservoir of strength and resilience that lies within you. Every trial, every tear, every moment of doubt has contributed to the fierce and radiant being you are today.

As we transition to our final chapter of the book, we'll delve into sealing your path to recovery, ensuring that you're not just moving on, but soaring, with a heart full of hope, wisdom, and an unquenchable spirit of renewal.

12

THE PHOENIX'S FLIGHT

A CONCLUSION AND A NEW BEGINNING

As we reach the culmination of our shared voyage through the Phoenix Path, I find it both essential and heartening to take a moment's pause and reflect on the vast expanse we've covered together. This book, dear reader, was penned with the deepest desire to guide you through the shadowed valleys and luminous peaks of recovery, to shine a light where darkness once dwelled.

We commenced our journey with the challenge of recognizing narcissism. Like the earliest twinges of dawn, this recognition began as a faint glimmer but grew brighter with understanding. Through my own story and the myriad stories of others, you found resonance, validation, and most importantly, awareness.

This awakening led us to delve into the intricate web of abuse, unraveling its threads and patterns. The stark clarity with which you began to discern manipulation, gaslighting, and emotional coercion became a testament to your growing insight.

Yet, as with any profound journey, there were times of reckoning, where you were called to face and acknowledge the impact of this abuse. A Phoenix's rebirth is not without its pain, and the transformation required you to acknowledge the scars, the wounds, and the toll taken. But in this acknowledgment lay the seeds of empowerment.

With understanding came a pivotal decision: the choice to change. Recognizing that the status quo was untenable, you showed immense courage, deciding to break free and reclaim your autonomy.

Once you stepped into that newfound freedom, the task of rebuilding life beckoned. It was akin to a Phoenix meticulously crafting its nest, preparing for its majestic rebirth. And as we explored together, this rebuilding was multifaceted, encompassing rediscovering identity, forging a support system, and establishing personal boundaries to protect your sacred space.

Our next ascent on this path was toward healing—both the mind and the spirit. Through introspection, therapy, mindfulness, and myriad self-care practices, you embarked on an inner pilgrimage, rediscovering the resilient Phoenix within, always rising, always enduring.

And as we approached the horizon, the topic of fostering healthy relationships surfaced. Equipped with the wisdom from past experiences, you learned to spot the red flags, to build relationships founded on respect, understanding, and genuine connection.

Your journey has been nothing short of extraordinary. From the ashes of pain and confusion, you've risen, and now you soar with strength, wisdom, and a heart open to love and healthy connections.

Remember, this little recap is not just a mere reflection of pages read but of a life transformed, a spirit rejuvenated, and a future reclaimed.

Growth and resilience are intertwined, much like the roots and branches of an ancient tree. One provides the foundation, while the other reaches for the skies, both essential in the grand tapestry of life. And just as a tree faces storms, droughts, and seasons of change, so too does our journey of healing.

Healing is much like the river's course. There are times it flows serenely, peaceful and steady. But there will also be moments of tumultuous rapids, where you might feel you've been thrust back into the turbulent waters of the past. It's crucial to remember: healing is not linear. There is no prescriptive path or timetable that dictates your progress. Setbacks, while challenging, are a natural part of the journey. They are not failures, but rather signposts, illuminating areas that require a deeper understanding or care.

The lessons from this book, the insights you've gleaned, and the strategies you've embraced, are not just for a phase but for a lifetime. Each chapter, each exercise, and each reflection is a tool in your arsenal. As life evolves, as challenges emerge, revisit these pages. They are your anchor, a reminder of the Phoenix spirit that dwells within.

However, know that you are not alone in this flight. Your wings, no matter how powerful, may sometimes tire. In those moments, it's not just okay, but imperative, to seek support. Whether through therapy, trusted friends, support groups, or communities that resonate with your experiences, allow yourself the grace to lean on others when the weight feels too heavy.

The Phoenix, in all its splendor, does not rise just once. It rises again and again, each time from the ashes, each time with greater luminance. Your journey, too, is marked by these continuous risings. Celebrate your progress, recognize the power of your resilience, and know that with each dawn, you're given another opportunity to soar even higher.

Emerging from the shadow of narcissistic abuse is akin to stepping into the warm embrace of the sun after enduring a prolonged, cold winter. The transition isn't without its pains – the thawing of frostbitten parts can sting – yet, with time, the sun's nurturing glow bestows upon us strength, clarity, and growth.

Living a fulfilling life after such trauma requires intention, patience, and above all, self-compassion. It's about reclaiming your identity, rediscovering your passions, and rekindling the fire that once may have felt extinguished. Every sunrise you've witnessed, every step you've taken forward, serves as a testament to your unyielding spirit.

In your journey ahead, as you navigate the vast landscape of life, let the following guiding principles serve as your compass, especially in moments clouded by doubt or difficulty:

1. Self-Compassion is Key: Treat yourself with the same kindness and understanding as you would a dear friend. Remember that healing is personal, and everyone's timeline is unique.

2. Boundaries are Sacred: These are your protective barriers, reflecting your self-worth and ensuring your well-being. They are to be honored and respected, both by you and those around you.

3. Growth is Continuous: Much like the Phoenix, every end is a new beginning. Every experience, even the most challenging ones, offers lessons that contribute to your evolution.

4. Seek Connection: While solitude can offer profound insights, remember the power of connectedness. Reach out, share, listen, and

let the tapestry of human experiences enrich your life.

5. Trust Your Intuition: Your inner compass, sharpened by past experiences, is a powerful guide. Trust its nudges, its whispers, and sometimes its alarms.

6. Celebrate Small Wins: Every step, no matter how minor it might seem, is a victory in its own right. Acknowledge them, for they compound into significant transformation over time.

As you turn each page of your life's chapter, envision your story through the eyes of the Phoenix: a magnificent creature that rises from adversity with even more brilliance. Your narrative, marked by challenges but defined by resilience, is one of hope, growth, and boundless potential. Always remember, the horizon holds promises waiting to be embraced, and you have the wings to reach them.

As you stand at this crossroads, having traversed the tumultuous terrain of narcissistic abuse and healing, it's crucial to continuously nourish the roots of your recovery and fortify your spirit for the journey ahead. Here are some potential steps and resources to consider, ensuring your flight remains elevated and your path illuminated:

Potential Next Steps:

1. Therapeutic Support: Engage in individual therapy with a professional who specializes in trauma and narcissistic abuse. This provides a safe space to process emotions, heal wounds, and strategize for future well-being.

2. Join Support Groups: Being part of a community where members share similar experiences can be profoundly healing. Such groups offer a sense of belonging, understanding, and collective wisdom.

3. Further Reading: Expand your knowledge on the topic. Books offer in-depth insights, strategies, and narratives that can provide additional guidance and validation.

4. Engage in Mindfulness Practices: Techniques such as meditation, journaling, and yoga can deepen your connection with yourself, offer clarity, and enhance emotional regulation.

5. Attend Workshops and Seminars: Participate in events focused on recovery, self-improvement, and personal growth. They can introduce you to new tools, perspectives, and networks of support.

Resources:

Books:

- "The Narcissistic Family: Diagnosis and Treatment" by Stephanie Donaldson-Pressman and Robert M. Pressman
- "Will I Ever Be Good Enough? Healing the Daughters of Narcissistic Mothers" by Dr. Karyl McBride

Websites:

- Out of the Fog (https://www.outofthefog. website/): A resource for those with a family member or loved one who suffers from a personality disorder.
- The Narcissistic Abuse Recovery Program (https://www.melanietoniaevans.com/): An extensive range of articles, webinars, and recovery programs.

Hotlines:

- National Domestic Violence Hotline: Available 24/7 for guidance and support. Call 1-800-799-SAFE (7233).
- Crisis Text Line: For immediate assistance, text HOME to 741741.

Remember, as you continue on your path, each resource you tap into, every step you take, serves to fortify your Phoenix spirit. The world is rich with tools and support; it's just a matter of reaching out and harnessing them to further elevate your journey.

Dear Phoenix,

As we bring this journey to a close, I want to acknowledge the tremendous courage, strength, and resilience you've displayed by embarking on and persisting through the Phoenix Path. Every page you turned, every insight you gleaned, and every tear you shed, served as testament to your unyielding commitment to healing, growth, and transformation.

Remember, just like the mythical Phoenix, you have risen from the ashes, rejuvenated and renewed, ready to soar into a future filled with promise and potential. The challenges you faced, the pain you endured, didn't diminish your light but rather fueled your ascent, illuminating your path towards self-realization.

The core message of this book, and the essence of your journey, is empowerment and resilience. Life may have presented you with trials that seemed insurmountable, but here you stand, not just a survivor, but a thriver, embodying the Phoenix's spirit.

I want to thank you. Thank you for trusting this guide, for believing in the process, and most importantly, for believing in yourself. The journey of recovery, as you've seen, is not a straight path, but a mosaic of experiences, each piece contributing to the larger, beautiful picture of your life.

And as you soar higher, remember, your story has the power to guide, uplift, and inspire others. By sharing your experiences and learnings, you become a beacon of hope for those still trapped in the shadows of narcissistic abuse. Your journey could light the way for others, showing them that they, too, possess the Phoenix's indomitable spirit, waiting to rise and soar.

In the tapestry of life, we are all interconnected, threads of shared experiences and lessons. By weaving your story into this grand design, you contribute to a narrative of hope, resilience, and rebirth.

Fly high, dear Phoenix. The horizon beckons, and the skies are limitless.

With deepest admiration and gratitude,

Dr. Emily Clark.

A Personal Request from the Author

As a self-published author, your feedback means the world to me. Hearing from readers like you not only helps me grow as a writer but also helps other people find this resource when they need it most. If you found "The Phoenix Path" helpful, I would be incredibly grateful if you could take a few moments to leave an honest review on Amazon. Your words could guide other people to the support and strategies they need to empower themselves to rise. Your voice truly matters and can make a difference in the lives of other people. Thank you from the bottom of my heart for your support and for joining me on this journey. Together, we are building a community of individuals freed from the grasp of narcissistic abuse, fostering healthier and more harmonious personal relationships.

Scan to leave an honest review

ABOUT THE AUTHOR

Dr. Emily Clark is a highly respected clinical psychologist with over twenty years of experience specializing in personality disorders and emotional abuse recovery. With a Ph.D. in Clinical Psychology from Stanford University, she has dedicated her professional life to helping individuals regain their sense of self after enduring narcissistic abuse.

After witnessing the widespread need for accessible and practical tools for abuse victims, she wrote "The Phoenix Path: Rising from the Ashes of Narcissistic Abuse" to empower readers with the knowledge and strategies to escape toxic relationships and rebuild their lives.

Drawing from her rich experience in working with survivors of narcissistic abuse, Dr. Clark has a deep understanding of the pain and confusion that victims often experience. Her compassionate approach is felt in her writing as she guides readers through their healing journey, offering evidence-based advice combined with encouraging affirmations and self-reflection prompts.

In addition to her book, Dr. Clark also runs a successful therapy practice and provides workshops and seminars to promote understanding of narcissistic abuse and emotional healing. Her passion for helping others is a common thread in her work, and she is a firm believer in the power of resilience and self-love in overcoming adversity.

Her mission is to shine a light on narcissistic abuse, help victims understand that they are not alone, and give them the tools to rise into a life of strength, freedom, and self-love.

amazon.com/author/emily-clark

Unlock Your Full Healing Potential

Feeling inspired and ready for actionable steps?

Dive Deeper with Our Exclusive Course!

Introducing The Phoenix Path Course!

- 💼 Engaging, real-world strategies.
- 🤝 Connect with a compassionate community of fellow phoenixes.
- 🌱 Rise above past traumas with interactive lessons, healing exercises, and more!

> "After the book, this course became the guiding light I needed to actively begin my transformative journey." – Anna L.

LIMITED TIME OFFER

As a reader of Emily's profound book, you are exclusively eligible for a special offer!

Get $50 OFF when you enroll in the course today:

YOU GOT A VALUE
50$

COUPON CODE
50-OFF-COURSE

🔗 Ready to Transform?

Visit Our Link:
https://payhip.com/b/IZxkc

OR scan the QR code below

Don't just read about change – embrace it! Continue your journey with Emily and our supportive community today.

Made in the USA
Las Vegas, NV
19 January 2024

84592563R00100